More Praise for
Michael Eric Dyson
and *Tears We Cannot Stop*

Winner of the Southern Book Prize

"Everybody who speaks after Michael Eric Dyson pales in comparison."
—**President Barack Obama**

"Readers will find searing moments in *Tears We Cannot Stop*, when Dyson's words prove unforgettable. . . . But more than education, Dyson wants a reckoning."
—*The Washington Post*

"Be ready to pause nearly every other sentence, absorb what is said, and prepare for action. *Tears We Cannot Stop* is meant to change your thinking."
—*The Miami Times*

"Talks directly to you, about issues deep, disturbing, and urgently in need of being faced."
—**Philly.com**

"[Dyson's] narrative voice carries a deeper and more intimate authority, as it grows from his own experience as a black man in America. . . . "
—*The Chicago Tribune*

"Impassioned."
—*Library Journal*

"Dyson affirms his unique position at the intersection of scholarship and the public arena, in the halls of academe and the corridors of political power, in scholarly discourse and the most thoughtful journalism."

—Henry Louis Gates

"Anguish and hurt throb in every word."

—*The Philadelphia Inquirer*

"Dyson lays bare our conscience, then offers redemption through our potential change."

—*Booklist*

"At a time when everyone needs to speak more openly, honestly, and critically about the racial divisions that have been allowed to grow in the United States, Dyson's book . . . could not be a more welcome read."

—*Bustle*

"A hard-hitting sermon on the racial divide. . . . The readership Dyson addresses may not fully be convinced, but it can hardly remain unmoved."

—*Kirkus Reviews* (starred review)

"Michael Eric Dyson is alive to the fierce urgency of now and yet he's full of felicitous contradictions: an intellectual who won't talk down to anyone; a man of God who eschews piousness; a truth-teller who is not afraid of doubt or nuance; a fighter whose arguments, though always to the point, are never ad hominem."

**—Dave Eggers,
from the preface of *Can You Hear Me Now?***

"A world-class scholar."

—Jay Z

TEARS
WE
CANNOT
STOP

A Sermon to White America

MICHAEL ERIC DYSON

ST. MARTIN'S
GRIFFIN
NEW YORK

Published in the United States by St. Martin's Griffin, an imprint of
St. Martin's Publishing Group

www.stmartins.com

Library of Congress Cataloging-in-Publication Data

Names: Dyson, Michael Eric, author.
Title: Tears we cannot stop : a sermon to white America /
    Michael Eric Dyson.
Description: First edition. | New York : St. Martin's Press, 2017.
Identifiers: LCCN 2016049919 | ISBN 9781250135995 (hardcover) |
    ISBN 9781250776679 (paperback) | ISBN 9781250136008 (e-book)
Subjects: LCSH: United States—Race relations. | African Americans—
    Race identity. | Whites—Race identity—United States. |
    Whites—United States—Attitudes. | Racism—United States. |
    Race discrimination—United States. | Race relations—Religious
    aspects—Christianity.
Classification: LCC E185.615 .D976 2017 | DDC 305.800973—dc23
LC record available at https://lccn.loc.gov/2016049919

First St. Martin's Griffin Edition: 2021

10 9 8 7 6 5 4 3 2 1

To

Beyoncé Knowles Carter
Lover of Black People
Genius and Greatest Living Entertainer
Feminist and Global Humanitarian

Solange Knowles
Lover of Black People
Amazing Artist
Fearless Advocate for the Vulnerable

Tina Knowles-Lawson
Lover of Black People
Gifted Fashion Designer and Philanthropist
Loving Matriarch

What it comes to is that if we, who can scarcely be considered a white nation, persist in thinking of ourselves as one, we condemn ourselves, with the truly white nations, to sterility and decay, whereas if we could accept ourselves as we are, we might bring new life to the Western achievements, and transform them . . . The price of this transformation is the unconditional freedom of the Negro . . . He is the key figure in his country, and the American future is precisely as bright or as dark as his.

—James Baldwin

CONTENTS

I. Call to Worship   1

II. Hymns of Praise   9

III. Invocation   19

IV. Scripture Reading   35

V. Sermon   41

Repenting of Whiteness   43
  1. Inventing Whiteness, 44
  2. The Five Stages of White Grief, 71
  3. The Plague of White Innocence, 95

Being Black in America   125
  4. Nigger, 126
  5. Our Own Worst Enemy? 143
  6. Coptopia, 170

VI. Benediction   195

VII. Offering Plate   213

VIII. Prelude to Service   217

IX. Closing Prayer   225

Sunday School Lessons   229

I.

CALL TO WORSHIP

"Here," she said, "in this here place, we flesh; flesh that weeps, laughs; flesh that dances on bare feet in grass. Love it. Love it hard. Yonder they do not love your flesh. They despise it. They don't love your eyes; they'd just as soon pick em out. No more do they love the skin on your back. Yonder they flay it . . . And no, they ain't in love with your mouth. Yonder, out there, they will see it broken and break it again. What you say out of it they will not heed. What you scream from it they do not hear."

—Toni Morrison, *Beloved*

America is in trouble, and a lot of that trouble—perhaps most of it—has to do with race. Everywhere we turn, there is discord and division, death and destruction. When we survey the land, we see a country full of suffering that we cannot fully understand, and a history that we can no longer deny. Slavery casts a long shadow across our lives. The spoils we reaped from forcing people to work without wages and treating them with grievous inhumanity continue to haunt us in a racial gulf that seems impossible to overcome. Black and white people don't merely have different experiences; we seem to occupy different universes, with worldviews that are fatally opposed to one another. The merchants of racial despair easily peddle their wares in a marketplace riddled by white panic and fear. Black despair piles up with each body that gets snuffed on video and streamed on social media. We have, in the span of a few years, elected the nation's first black president and placed in the Oval Office the scariest racial demagogue in a generation. The two may not be unrelated. The remarkable progress we seemed to make with the former has brought out the peril of the latter.

What, then, can we do? We must return to the moral and spiritual foundations of our country and grapple with the consequences of our original sin. To do that we need not share the same religion, worship the same God, or, truly, even be believers at all. For better and worse, our national moral landscape has been shaped by the dynamics

of a Christianity that has from the start been deeply intertwined with religious mythology and cultural symbolism.
The Founding Fathers did not for the most part believe what
evangelical Christians believe now. Most believers today certainly do not share Thomas Jefferson's view of the Bible. In
his redacted version of the New Testament, Jefferson purged
the miracles, Jesus' divinity, and the Resurrection. But all
of us, from agreeable agnostics to fire-and-brimstone Prot-
estants, from devout Catholics to observant Jews, from de-
voted Muslims to those who claim no god at all, share a
language of moral repair. That language is our common
meeting ground, our tool of analysis, and yes, our inspiration for repentance, our hope for redemption.

Although I am a scholar, a cultural and political critic,
and a social activist, I am, before, and above anything else,
an ordained Baptist minister. Please don't hold that against
me, although I'll understand if you do. I know that religion
has a bad rap. We believers deserve a lot of the criticism that
we receive. Our actions and beliefs nearly warrant wholesale
skepticism. (Can I let you in on a secret? I share a lot of that
reaction, but that's another book.) But deep in my heart
I believe that our moral and spiritual passions can lead to
a better day for our nation. I know that when we get out
of our own way and let the spirit of love and hope shine
through we are a better people.

But such love and hope can only come about if we first
confront the poisonous history that has almost unmade our
nation and undone our social compact. We must face up to
what we as a country have made of the black people who
have been the linchpin of democracy, the folk who saved

America from itself, who redeemed it from the hypocrisy of proclaiming liberty and justice for all while denying all that liberty and justice should be to us.

Yes, I said us. This is where I take leave of my analytical neutrality, or at least the appearance of it. This is where I cast my fate with the black people who birthed and loved me, who built a legacy of excellence and struggle and pride amidst one of the most vicious assaults on humanity in recorded history. That assault may have started with slavery, but it didn't end there. The legacy of that assault, its lingering and lethal effect, continues to this day. It flares in broken homes and blighted communities, in low wages and social chaos, in self-destruction and self-hate too. But so much of what ails us—black people, that is—is tied up with what ails you—white folk, that is. We are tied together in what Martin Luther King, Jr., called a single garment of destiny. Yet sewed into that garment are pockets of misery and suffering that seem to be filled with a disproportionate number of black people. (Of course, America is far from simply black and white by whatever definition you use, but the black-white divide has been the major artery through which the meaning of race has flowed throughout the body politic.)

Now just because I identify with my people doesn't mean that I don't understand and grapple with what it means to be white in America. In fact, I was trained in your schools and I now teach your children. But I remain what I was when I started my vocation, my pilgrimage of self-discovery: a black preacher. It is for that reason that I don't want to—really, I can't afford to—give up on the possibility that white America can definitively, finally, hear from one black American preacher a plea, a cry, a sermon, from my heart to yours.

If you're interested in my social analysis and my scholarly reflections on race, I've written plenty of other books for you to read. I tried to make this book one of them, but in the end, I couldn't. I kept coming up short. I kept deleting words from the screen, a lot of them, enough of them to drive me to despair that I'd ever finish. I was stopped cold. I was trying to make the message fit the form, when it was the form itself that was the problem.

What I need to say can only be said as a sermon. I have no shame in that confession, because confession, and repentance, and redemption play a huge role in how we can make it through the long night of despair to the bright day of hope. Sermons are tough, not only to deliver, but, just as often, to hear. Yet, in my experience, if we stick with the sermon—through its pitiless recall of our sin, its relentless indictment of our flaws—we can make it to the uplifting expressions and redeeming practices that make our faith flow from the pulpit to the public, from darkness to light.

There is a long tradition of a kind of sermon, or what some call the jeremiad, an extended lamentation about the woes we face, about the woes we embody, a mournful catalogue of complaint, the blues on page or stage. Henry David Thoreau was a friend to the form; so was Martin Luther King, Jr. Instead of blasting the nation from outside the parameters of its moral vision, the jeremiad, named after the biblical prophet Jeremiah, comes calling from within. It calls us to reclaim our more glorious features from the past.

It calls us to relinquish our hold on—really, to set ourselves free from—the dissembling incarnations of our faith, our country, and democracy itself that thwart the vision that set us on our way. To repair the breach by announcing it first, and then saying what must be done to move forward.

I offer this sermon to you, my dear white friends, my beloved comrades of faith and country. My sermon to you is cast in the form of a church service. I adopt the voices of the worship and prayer leader, the choir director, the reader of scripture, the giver of testimony, the preacher of the homily, the bestower of benediction and the exhorter to service, and the collector of the offering plate. I do so in the interest of healing our nation through honest, often blunt, talk. It will make you squirm in your seat with discomfort before, hopefully, pointing a way to relief.

I do not do so from a standpoint of arrogance, of being above the fray, pointing the finger without an awareness of my own frailty, my own suffering and need for salvation. And yet I must nevertheless prophesy, not because I'm perfect, but because I'm called. God stood in my way when I tried to write anything, and everything, except what I offer you now.

This is written to you, my friends, because I feel led by the Spirit to preach to you. I don't mind if you call Spirit common sense, or desperate hope, or willful refusal to accept defeat. I don't mind if you conclude that religion is cant and faith is a lie. I simply want to bear witness to the truth I see and the reality I know. And without white America wrestling with these truths and confronting these realities, we may not survive. To paraphrase the Bible, to whom much is given, much is required. And you, my friends, have been given so much. And the Lord knows, what wasn't given, you simply took, and took, and took. But the time is at hand for reckoning with the past, recognizing the truth of the present, and moving together to redeem the nation for our future. If we don't act now, if you don't address race immediately, there very well may be no future.

II.
HYMNS OF PRAISE

What are these songs, and what do they mean? . . . They are the music of an unhappy people, of the children of disappointment; they tell of death and suffering and unvoiced longing toward a truer world.

—W.E.B. Du Bois

My ten-year-old son Mike was visiting my wife and me in Hartford, Connecticut, during the summer of 1988. I was a teacher and assistant director of a poverty project at Hartford Seminary. One evening we all piled into the car to drive over to my office to pick up some papers. Mike was behaving so badly in the car that I pulled over to the side of the road and gave him three licks on his hands. I was a young parent who had grown up with licks of my own and hadn't yet learned the damage that corporal punishment wreaks. After I finished disciplining him I drove the single block to my building.

As I neared the seminary, two white cops drove up in their squad car. They signaled me to pull over before they got out of their vehicle. One of the cops approached my door, commanding me to get out of the car. His partner approached my wife's door.

"Can I ask you why you're stopping me, officer?" I asked politely and professionally. Like most black men I'd learned to be overly indulgent to keep the blue wrath from crashing on my head.

"Just get out of the car," he demanded.

As I opened the door, I told the cop that I was a professor at Hartford Seminary, pointing to the school behind me.

"Sure," he said drolly. "And I'm John Wayne."

Even before he instructed me, I knew to "assume the position," to place my hands against the car and lean forward.

I'd done it so many times I could offer a class on correct procedure. I could hear the other cop quizzing my wife, asking her if everything was okay, if my son was fine. Mike was in the back seat crying, fearful of what might happen to me.

"I'm fine, I'm fine," Mike tearfully insisted. "Why are you doing this to my dad?"

I heard snatches of the other cop's conversation with my wife. Obviously someone—a well-meaning white person no doubt—had seen me punishing Mike in the car and reported it as child abuse. I was ashamed that I had given licks to my son. I was embarrassed that my actions had brought the fury of the cops down on me, on us.

Just as my wife was telling the cop how preposterous this was, two more police cars pulled up with four more white cops.

Damn, I thought to myself, *if I had been mugged, I bet I couldn't have gotten a cop to respond within half an hour. And now, within five minutes of disciplining my son, I've got six cops breathing down my neck ready to haul me into the station for child abuse. Or worse.*

The other cops formed a circle around our car. The cop who pulled me from my car still refused to explain why he had stopped me. He forcefully patted me down as my wife and my son explained yet again that I had done nothing wrong and that Mike was fine.

"You sure everything's alright?" the cop asked my wife while looking my way for degrading emphasis. She angrily insisted that all was fine.

Finally the cop frisking me addressed me.

"We got a complaint that someone was hurting a child," he said.

"I can assure you that I love my son, and that I wasn't hurting him," I said in a measured voice. "I punished my child now so that he wouldn't one day end up being arrested by you," I couldn't help adding. And instantly I regretted my words, hoping my brief fit of snarkiness wouldn't set him off and get me hammered or shot.

"We have to check on these things," the second cop snapped back. "Just don't do anything wrong."

The cop frisking me proceeded to shove me against the car for good measure. Then the six cops got back into their cars and unsurprisingly offered no apology before driving off.

After I picked up my papers, I was still shaken up, and so was my family. Back in the car, I fast forwarded the tape of N.W.A.'s debut album, *Straight Outta Compton,* to "Fuck tha Police," their blunt and poetic war cry against unwarranted police aggression and terror. I cranked up the volume, blasting the song out of my car window. The FBI harassed N.W.A.; local police were enraged by their lyrics. But many of us felt that this song about brutality and profiling finally captured our rage against police terror.

I thought "fuck" seemed the right word for cops who bring terror on black folk.

The historian Edward E. Baptist reminds us that "fuck" is from the Old English word that means to strike or beat, and before that, to plow and tear open. The cops have fucked the lives of black folk.

✢   ✢   ✢

Beloved, as your choir director, I implore you to sing with me now. These hymns pronounce profane lyrical judgment on our unjust urban executioners. Some will be unfamiliar to you. But critical times call for critical hymns. These songs reflect our terror at the hands of the police in the strongest words possible. These are what our hymns sound like in America today. Therefore, as the old folk say, I will line out the hymn for you and give you the words of the tune as they are to be sung.

Our first hymnist is KRS-One, our generation's James Cleveland, the master composer of gospel songs. KRS-One wrote a wonderful song that captures our collective trauma. It is entitled "Sound of da Police."

Let me call out his words for you to repeat. "Yeah, officer from overseer you need a little clarity? / Check the similarity." Dear friends, in this song KRS-One argues that his grandfather, his great-grandfather, and his great-great-grandfather had to deal with the cops. KRS-One asks the question, and I ask you to sing along with me, "When's it gonna stop?!"

We will also sing another of KRS-One's splendid songs. It is entitled "Who Protects Us from You?" KRS-One says of the police: "You were put here to protect us / But who protects us from you?"

Let us turn our hymnals to our next song, composed by the Fugees, fronted by the powerful Lauryn Hill, who eventually left the group to find even greater applause as a solo artist. Think of her as you think of our beloved Aretha

Franklin, who was a member of the New Bethel Baptist Church choir in Detroit before she departed to achieve international stardom on her own. The Fugees wrote a powerful attack on police brutality entitled "The Beast." In it, Lauryn Hill raps that if she loses control because of the cops' psychological tricks then she will be sent to a penitentiary "such as Alcatraz, or shot up like El-Hajj Malik Shabazz . . . And the fuzz treat bruh's like they manhood never was."

The next hymn was composed by the great Tupac Shakur. He was one of the most influential artists of our time. Shakur began his career composing odes to the Black Panthers. He went on to embrace more universal inspirations before meeting a violent death on the streets of Las Vegas. Shakur brings to mind Sam Cooke, the legendary gospel artist who shifted gears and became a soul and pop star before he was violently shot down in Los Angeles. Let us perform together the words of Tupac's poignant hymn, "Point The Finga." In this song Tupac says that he had been lynched by crooked cops who retained their jobs, and that his tax dollars were subsidizing his own oppression by paying them to "knock the blacks out."

⊹   ⊹   ⊹

I teach the work of these hymnists at Georgetown, so my students can hear their lessons and perhaps change their tunes of social justice. We have pored over Jay Z's lyrics. Of course they hear his exaltation of hustling. But more important, they hear in his "A Ballad For The Fallen Soldier" a deep and angry battle with the police terror that grips black life.

Off to boot camp, the world's facing terror
Bin Laden been happenin' in Manhattan
Crack was anthrax back then, back when
Police was Al-Qaeda to black men.

And we also study Beyoncé. Many of you have danced to her feminist rhymes and absorbed her insistence that black life matters. That insistence rings out on her song "Formation," whose video features the songstress sitting atop a sinking cop car in the post-Katrina Louisiana bayou and a message scribbled on a wall that says, simply, plainly, unapologetically, "Stop Shooting Us." Beyoncé also sang the song during an epic Super Bowl halftime show, garbed in black, as were her fashionable phalanx of backup dancers, paying tribute to the Black Panthers. Many cops charged that she was anti-police and threatened to withdraw protection during her "Formation" tour. "Let's be clear: I am against police brutality and injustice," she told *Elle* magazine. "If celebrating my roots and culture during Black History Month made anyone uncomfortable, those feelings were there long before a video and long before me." On tour her radiant blackness and her ecumenical humanitarianism never once clashed.

We also study Kendrick Lamar. We listen to his racial catechism and thus absorb as well his subtle and stirring exploration of black life in all of its magnetic contradictions. We watch the black-and-white video for "Alright," a song of cataclysmic hope amidst cops' fiendish assaults on black men and women. The video unveils the uplifting dimensions of an urban magical realism. Lamar flies over hood landscapes until he lands on top of a high streetlight, only to be felled by the imaginary bullet spun from a cop's imaginary gun, a gun formed by the cop's pointing fingers. Kendrick falls in slow motion, dead, or at least we think he is. Then he opens his eyes and smiles widely. He lets us in on the joke, on the artifice of what we have just seen. It is, too, a stinging rejection of the power of blue to determine black life and death.

These are our griots. These are their songs. These and a thousand others are the hymns that answer the reign of terror that consumes our days. These are the hymns that rally us against the fantasy of our erasure. May these hymns be sung loud until our slaughter ceases and our blood no longer spills.

III.

INVOCATION

O! save us, we pray thee, thou God of Heaven and of
earth, from the devouring hands of the white
Christians!!!...
The whites have murder'd us, O God!...
We believe that, for thy glory's sake,
Thou wilt deliver us;
But that thou may'st effect these things,
Thy glory must be sought.

—David Walker

A lmighty, hear our prayer.

Oh God, how we suffer. We your servants are ensnared in tragedy that doesn't end. We can do nothing to make our tormentors stop their evil. We cannot convince them that we are your children and don't deserve this punishment. We have tried everything we can to keep them from slaughtering us in the streets. They hide behind the state to justify killing us. They say we are scary, that they are afraid for their lives. They say this even when we have nothing in our hands but air. They say this even when they are armed with weapons meant to remove us from the face of the earth. They say this even when they must throw down guns to pretend that we intended to do them harm. They say this even when video proves they are lying through their teeth.

Oh God, we are near complete despair. How can we possibly change our fate? How can we possibly persuade our society that we deserve to be treated with decency and respect? How can we possibly fight a criminal justice system that has been designed to ensure our defeat? How can we possibly combat the blindness of white men and women who are so deeply invested in their own privilege that they cannot afford to see how we much we suffer?

But most of all, Oh God, how can we keep racism from strangling every bit of hope left in our bodies and minds? How can we arrest the blue plague and keep it from spreading to our children, and our children's children? Oh God, I have already seen the tragic imprint of grief and suffering on my own children's fates. I have seen how the poison of racism has tried to claim their bodies and minds from the time they were babies.

✤　✤　✤

Oh God, I pray for all children who have to endure the curse of bigotry. It is the most wretched feeling of helplessness when one's children suffer that fate. My daughter Maisha was six years old the first time racism stole upon her. She had been invited to an ice skating party hosted by a dear childhood friend. Her friend's parents had moved the family from the inner city to a Chicago suburb. Yes, Oh God, you moved them on up like Weezie and George Jefferson. Maisha was delighted to see her old schoolmate. She was equally excited to get a taste of the suburbs. The group of kids that attended the party spanned the black rainbow from pale vanilla to dark chocolate. A few of the girls decided to break away from the group and play a game on the ice. As they huddled in a circle, three white girls between the ages of six and ten approached them.

I know they're your creatures, too, Lord, but sometimes white folk act like the Devil is all in them. The Holy Ghost is nowhere in the vicinity. Well on this occasion the white girls yelled at my daughter and her friends in unison, "Move, niggers!"

Lord, Maisha was stopped in her tracks. She squinted her little green eyes to make sure that she'd truly heard what she thought she heard. The oldest girl in Maisha's circle demanded, "What did you just say?" And those lovely little minions, with no hesitation, with the kind of confidence that whiteness offers in spades, blurted out again, "Move, niggers!"

Maisha's heart sank.

And then it started. The predictable questions that hate provokes, all the self-doubt that racism means to implant. Do we know them? What did we do to deserve that? Why did they call us that horrible name?

You made her, Oh Lord. You know that Maisha's little mind drifted off into a faraway place. You know she sought to deflect the pain she felt. But she was snatched back into a crude reality. It was a hell of a way for her to be introduced to the ugliness and nastiness that racism unleashes. But there is never a good time to be hated because of a small and insignificant thing like the color of your skin. There is never a good time to know that for many white folk your blackness makes you Old Lucifer himself. There is never a good time to realize that your childhood is gone, that it has been rudely taken away by something as simple as a word, a stupid, nasty, filthy, little word. *Nigger.*

By that time the oldest black girl harked up a mouthful of spit. For the occasion it may as well have been holy water. Lord, it should have been regarded as Holy Communion. The saliva in her throat was transmuted from mere water to divine disgust. That blessed angel of a child planted her feet and then showered those white girls with her liquid resentment. I swear that may have been the biggest miracle since you turned water to wine.

I don't usually approve of such displays of raw anger. I usually counsel taking the higher road. But I must confess, Oh Lord, that the lower road was just fine that day. Because that was the day precious little Maisha was forced to learn what race meant. That was the day she got an inkling that the world is ruined with tribal loyalties and caste systems and blood oaths pettier than any grudge that children might hold. This was different. This was lethal. The havoc that grownups wreak is always more costly. That episode wore on her for a long spell. But racism is nothing if not persistent and cyclical. It came back to my daughter again a couple of years later.

When she was eight years old, Maisha received a wonderful gift. She tagged along with a close family friend and her two daughters for a private tour of Disney World. Maisha was incredibly excited. It was her first time in Florida. She got a kick out of pronouncing the nearby town of Kissimmee because it contained the word "kiss." After Maisha and her two little companions settled into their modest hotel in Kissimmee, they begged the girls' mother to let them go downstairs to the pool immediately. It was a luxury they didn't have back home; they were just grateful to be in a warm climate away from the chilly winds of Chicago.

The girls plunged into the deep end of the pool. They played mermaids. They played Marco Polo. They pretended to be water gymnasts.

The girls finally took a brief break from play and parked themselves on the pool stairs. Just then the cutest little girl swam their way. She had the biggest blue eyes and natural blonde hair. When she got a gander at Maisha and her two friends, the little girl exclaimed in a matter-of-fact tone, "Niggers." The girls straightened their backs and screwed up their faces in disbelief. The little white girl stood up in disbelief too, perhaps amazed at the power of her single utterance to evoke such dramatic response. For a moment, they all froze. Maisha and her friends were in shock.

And then, spontaneously, they all burst out in laughter. It was an all-too-familiar gesture of self-defense. It was a way to stave off the creep of hate inside your brain.

This is what race hate does to our kids. It often attacks them without warning. It makes them develop a tough exterior to combat the flow of racial insanity into their minds. Thank you, Lord, that Maisha and her friends were wise enough —yes, Lord, a wisdom that only some children in this country have to possess at such an early age —to know that the little white girl was repeating what she heard, that she was reflecting what she'd been taught. Lessons of race that are learned early are hard to get rid of later on. Often they harden into warped perceptions of black folk. Those perceptions turn to cudgels that are wielded against us when we least expect it.

Lord, Maisha has grown into a brilliant woman of haunting beauty. Thank you for that. She now lives in Miami. But the impact of race remains. Maisha's fair skin makes her appear to be what the film and television industry terms "ethnically ambiguous." Last year she left her apartment late one evening to have a quiet dinner near the water. She listened to music on her iPhone to make her nine-block stroll more enjoyable. Maisha turned onto a usually quiet street. But on this night a few more folk were on the block, likely getting off work at one of the nearby hotels. Suddenly a guy was walking behind her talking loudly on his phone. She soon figured out he must be a black man when she heard him say, "Nah, Bruh, I just got off and I'm trying to relax and chill." That vernacular was like a letter from home. Maisha chuckled as she thought to herself, *Yeah man, I feel you!*

As Maisha made a sharp left turn onto a side street, a white man ran toward her with his arms flailing as if to warn her. Maisha ripped out her ear buds, wondering out loud if he was okay. "Yes," he exclaimed. "But I don't know if you realized it, but there was a black man walking behind you!" Maisha furrowed her pretty brow. She was doubly irritated. The man didn't realize that she's black. And most annoyingly he believed the black man's skin immediately made him a suspect. "Yeah?!" Maisha responded. "He had to be a threat just because he was walking, breathing, and black?!"

That's my girl. She knew, like I know, like most black folk know, that such fear is what gets black folk killed. After all, this is the same state where 17-year-old Trayvon Martin lost his life to a bigoted zealot who was suspicious of Trayvon because, well, he was Trayvon, because a person like him could exist, but shouldn't have existed, not in that neighborhood on that day.

✢   ✢   ✢

Oh Lord, this is my great fear for my children, for Maisha, and for Michael, and for Mwata, and for my grandchildren too. I am fearful that some smart-assed hotshot with a badge and a gun will thrill himself to the slow letting of blood from one of my children's bodies while he blithely ignores their suffering to high-five his sworn "to protect and serve" compatriot in crime. I am sorely afraid that some snap of racist judgment—which, by now, means that it will be justified as rational assessment under threatening circumstances, circumstances that our color always provokes—will cause the hair trigger of some cop's weapon to fire fury at my children.

Don't let it happen, Lord, please don't let it happen. Oh Lord, I cannot bear the thought of seeing another black person perish because of the weaponized fear and armed hostility of a society that hates black folk in its guts. It can happen to any of us. It can happen to all of us. That is why we are all scared, Lord.

✣   ✣   ✣

My oldest son, Mwata, is an anesthesiologist who lives in New York. My three children have six degrees, two of them from Ivy League schools. But that is no protection, Lord. Sometimes it even incites anger and resentment. Black success often breeds white rage. Black educational advance will not keep a cop with a terminal degree of black revulsion from aiming his ignorance at my children's bodies.

A couple of years ago Mwata and his oldest son, Mosi, went looking in New Jersey for a Mother's Day gift for Mosi's mother, Wanda. Mwata had clocked out of work in Brooklyn in mid-afternoon to pick up Mosi from his after school program in Queens. Mwata didn't own a car at the time so he rented a Zipcar for the day. Mwata and Mosi set out at five o'clock, seeking to avoid getting snarled in traffic. Mwata consulted an app on his phone to chart the quickest route. He placed his phone on the dashboard to avoid getting a ticket for driving and talking on a cell phone. When he made a right turn onto a street in Harlem, the phone slipped from the dashboard and fell to the floor. As he retrieved the phone, the glare in the dark must have attracted the attention of a cop. Mwata could see the flashing lights from a squad car behind him. He heard the command from the cop's loudspeaker to pull his car over. Mwata was afraid that he had run a stop sign that he didn't see.

A white cop, about 5'9" and in his early forties, approached the car and asked to see Mwata's driver's license. He offered no reason for stopping my son. The cop went back to his car for about ten minutes before returning to Mwata, who asked the policeman why he pulled him over. "It's illegal to drive and talk on a cell phone at the same time in New York," the cop replied. Mwata said that even though he had a Washington, D.C., driver's license, the law certainly made sense. "However, officer, I wasn't talking on the phone, nor was I texting, for that matter."

I have always impressed on Mwata the need to be extra courteous and not to in any way rile up the police. It is often an exercise in humiliation, one that white folk barely have to think about, but one that can mean the difference between life and death for us. Mwata tried to make nice with the cop. He informed him that as a physician he had spent many years as a member of trauma teams in Chicago,

Phoenix, and New York. He told him he was well aware of the dangers of multitasking while operating a vehicle. He said that he had saved, and unfortunately lost, many lives because of tragic car accidents. Mwata told the cop that his phone had slipped to the floor and he simply picked it up. Now Mosi, who had fallen asleep, began to stir.

The policeman went back and forth with Mwata about driving and talking, and Mwata kept politely insisting that he had broken no law. The cop was growing more belligerent and insulting. Still, Mwata tied to placate him by speaking in measured tones. It didn't help. He even showed the cop a police benevolent association card with the name and cell phone number of a cop he had just treated a couple of days earlier. The cop told Mwata the policeman on the card wasn't in his precinct. He coldly said it meant nothing to him. The cop grew more agitated as he tried to extract from Mwata a confession that he had broken the law. He took a couple of steps away from the car and ominously placed his hand on his gun.

Every time I think of it, Oh Lord, I shudder. The cop asked Mwata a question that haunts him to this day. He asked, nastily, hatefully, if Mwata were stupid.

You crafted Mwata in his mother's womb, God. You know him inside out. You know the quiet anger my son felt at having acquired a world-class education only to be questioned about his intelligence by a white boy whose IQ translated to an Intimidation Quotient provided by a shield that allowed him to mow down smart *niggers* with impunity. When Mwata said he didn't know what he meant, and wondered aloud why he asked such a question, the cop got even more agitated. He snapped that he should take Mwata to jail and that my son had no right to be driving a car. He shouted that if his son weren't with him that he'd have no problem placing Mwata in handcuffs and locking him up. The cop admitted that the only thing that was stopping him was that he had no place to put the five-year-old. That may have saved Mwata from certain arrest and—who knows?— maybe from an unjust, untimely death.

It was at that moment that the force of everything rained down on Mwata. The cop's tone was threatening, his hand was on his gun, and Mosi had awakened from sleep to see his father being disrespected and threatened by an officer of the law. Fear struck Mwata hard. He glanced at his son in the rearview mirror and had one thought.

I don't want to die tonight. I don't want my son to see me shot.

That brings tears to my eyes even as I chant this prayer. Even as I ask you, Oh God, to give me the strength to soldier on. What a chilling recognition of the high cost for such a simple offense, all because an enraged white male cop was feeling his oats and seeking to humiliate my son. All because he could get away with it. Even if my son had been guilty, his crime wouldn't have merited the implied threat of lethal force.

Mwata continued the dance of complete compliance. He nodded his head in agreement with the cop, doing anything he could not to be cut down in front of Mosi, my grandson, who, earlier that day, had been chosen to go to the principal's office to recite the Pledge of Allegiance over the loudspeaker for the entire school. The bitter paradox wasn't lost on Mwata or me when I heard the story.

The officer gave Mwata a ticket and a stern warning that if he ever saw him again he would take him straight to jail. He also insisted that Mwata park the car and not drive again that night. Literally five seconds after he let Mwata go the cop pulled over another black motorist. So many whites say they hate the quotas they associate with affirmative action, but quotas don't seem to bother the white folk in blue who can't get enough of them as they harass one black citizen after another.

To this day my grandson is worried every time he sees a cop. He fears the cops will try to arrest him and his father. He can't understand why the color of his skin is a reason to be targeted by the police. Mosi is only seven years old.

Lord, what are we to do?

When I look at Mosi and my other grandchildren, Layla and Maxem, all beautiful, all bright, all full of life, I swear to you, Oh Lord, it fills me with fear, and then anger, and grief, to think that some son of a bitch with a badge and a gun could just take their lives, take our lives, as if it means nothing. I am beyond rage, Oh Lord, at the utter complicity of even good white folk who claim that they care, and yet their voices don't ring out loudly and consistently against an injustice so grave that it sends us to our graves with frightening frequency. They wring their hands in frustration to prove that they empathize with our plight—that is, those who care enough to do so—and then throw them up in surrender.

What we mostly hear is deafening silence. What we mostly see is crushing indifference. Lord, what are we to do in a nation of people who claim to love you and hold fast to your word and way and yet they let their brothers and sisters murder us like we are animals?

Lord, Dear Lord, I don't want to feel this way, but I swear to you I want to kill dead any Godforsaken soul who thinks that killing black people is an acceptable price to pay for keeping this nation safe. But then, am I any better than that soul?

I am reminded, Oh Lord, of the modern parable of the chicken and pig having a conversation about each making a contribution to breakfast. They are stopped short when they realize that their contributions aren't equally demanding, won't have the same consequence. All the chicken has to do to make a good breakfast is lay an egg. But the pig has to give his behind to make bacon. He has to die.

Lord, Oh Lord, I am so tired—we are so tired—of being the pigs. We are tired of having to sacrifice our hides to feed America. That may help explain why some black folk take special delight in referring to the cops as pigs. We want them to share our grief, to feel our pain, if just a little of it, in a term they find offensive. But if they think that insult is abominable, if the reference is disrespectful, can they not imagine, Oh Lord, what it means to be the pig, to surrender life to fill the bellies of a nation that eats our souls and culture while excreting us as so much waste?

Lord, convict this nation as never before. Let our lives testify to your majesty, your love, your grace—and may this land know your displeasure, taste your holy wrath, for

killing us like pigs without conscience. Let this nation repent of its murderous ways. Only then will we even believe
that white folk know the God who plants a foot on earth
and regulates the wheel of time and circumstance. Until
then, Oh Lord, give us the courage to tell the truth to white
folk who need it more than air itself—who, we pray, will
come to hunger for it more than they hunger for our death.

IV.

SCRIPTURE READING

Do you know that a lot of the race problem grows out of the . . . need that some people have to feel superior. A need that some people have to feel . . . that their white skin ordained them to be first.

—Martin Luther King, Jr.

BOOK OF MARTIN LUTHER KING, JR.,
1968: 3–8

Martin Luther King, Jr., is the most quoted black man on the planet. His words are like scripture to you and, yes, to us too. His name is evoked, his speech referenced, during every racial crisis we confront. He has become the language of race itself. He is, too, the history of black America in a dark suit. But he is more than that. He is the struggle and suffering of our people distilled to a bullet in Memphis. King's martyrdom made him less a man, more a symbol, arguably a civic deity. But there are perils to hero-worship. His words get plucked from their original contexts, his ideas twisted beyond recognition. America has washed the grit from his rhetoric.

Beloved, you say you love King, or at least admire him, but you don't really know him, not the King who was too black and too radical for most of America. King drank from roots deep in black culture. He bathed in black language. He sprang from a black moral womb. Black teachers and preachers shaped King. They gave him fuel for his journey and the inspiration to change the world. King told the truth about you in black America, to black America, in ways he couldn't tell you. He said the toughest things about you in sacred black spaces. He did it because he felt safe with us. He did that to let us know that he knew what we were up against. He did it to let us know we weren't crazy. If the most celebrated black man on the globe could feel the way he did, then we had every right to feel the same way. That didn't make King a Janus-faced liar. He was, instead, a man of noble forbearance. He understood what white folk could hear; he knew what you dared not listen to. He knew what you could bear to know. He understood the white psyche and when and how to pressure you to do the right thing.

Early in his career King believed in the essential goodness of white America. He trusted most whites to put away their bigotry in the face of black suffering. In the last three years of his life he grew far more skeptical of the ability or willingness of white folk to change. He concluded, sadly, that most whites are unconscious racists. In sermon after sermon before black congregations, King lashed out at American racism. I know his words may surprise many of you. You may be tempted to dismiss them as the rants of a man gone off course, of a soul made black by bitterness. But they are the words of the greatest American prophet. This is civic Holy Writ; this is political scripture. They are the sentiments of the man whose carefully selected words grace his national memorial and fill the innocuous speeches of countless dignitaries. King's soul was indeed black, but it was made beautifully black by the culture that produced him, a culture of proud, loving, loyal, complicated blackness, a blackness that is often hidden from mainstream view even to this day.

Let us now read from the Book of King.

"Our nation was born in genocide when it embraced the doctrine that the original American, the Indian, was an inferior race," King said. "Even before there were large numbers of Negroes on our shores, the scar of racial hatred had already disfigured colonial society." We are "perhaps the only nation which tried as a matter of national policy to wipe out its indigenous population."

In 1968 King said the Constitution and the Declaration of Independence were penned by men who owned slaves, thus, a "nation that got started like that . . . has a lot of repenting to do." Before his own Atlanta congregation in 1968 King declared that for black folk the Declaration of Independence "has never had any real meaning in terms of implementation in our lives."

King said that black folk couldn't trust America and compared us to the Japanese who had been interned in concentration camps in World War II. "And you know what, a nation that put as many Japanese in a concentration camp as they did in the forties . . . will put black people in a concentration camp. And I'm not interested in being in any concentration camp. I been on the reservation too long now." Here King reverted to black vernacular to forge his link with the black folk whose comfort he sought as he got blasted in white America for criticizing the Vietnam War and for fighting to get rid of inequality. King concluded that black suffering has generated a "terrible ambivalence in the soul of white America."

In 1966 King said in Mississippi that our nation "has a choice. Either you give the Negro his God-given rights and his freedom or you face the fact of continual social disruption and chaos. America, which will you choose?" In 1967 King also declared that the "fact is that there has never been any single, solid, determined commitment on the part of the vast majority of white Americans . . . to genuine equality for Negroes." And just two weeks before his death, he announced, with a broken heart, "Yes it is true . . . America is a racist country."

That is why King is important to this generation, to this time, to this nation, to our people. He spoke the truth that we have yet to fully acknowledge.

V.
SERMON

[T]he destiny of the Negroes is in some measure interwoven with that of the Europeans. These two races are fastened to each other without intermingling; and they are alike unable to separate entirely or to combine. The most formidable of all the ills that threaten the future of the Union arises from the presence of a black population upon its territory; and in contemplating the cause of the present embarrassments, or the future dangers of the United States, the observer is invariably led to this as a primary fact.

—Alexis de Tocqueville

REPENTING OF

WHITENESS

1.

INVENTING WHITENESS

Beloved, let me start by telling you an ugly secret: there is no such thing as white people. And yet so many of them, so many of you, exist. Please hear me out. I know you're flesh and blood. I know that you use language and forks and knives. I'm not talking about your bodies or your garages or your grocery stores. I'm talking about the politics of whiteness. I'm talking about an identity that exists apart from the skin you're born in. I'm talking about a meaning of race that supersedes the features you inherit when you come out of the womb. You don't get whiteness from your genes. It is a social inheritance that is passed on to you as a member of a particular group.

And it's killing us, and, quiet as it's kept, it's killing you too.

Race has no meaning outside of the cultures we live in and the worlds we fashion out of its force and energy. Whiteness is an advantage and privilege because you have made it so, not because the universe demands it.

So I want to tell you right off the bat that whiteness is made up, and that white history disguised as American history is a fantasy, as much a fantasy as white superiority and white purity. Those are all myths. They're intellectual rubbish, cultural garbage. The quicker you accept that, the better off you'll be, and so will the rest of us.

Yes, yes, I know many of you are proud to be Irish, or Italian, or Polish, or Jewish. And those ethnic groups are as real as any other groups with identifiable cultures, languages, and histories. But when your ancestors got to America, they endured a profound makeover. All of your polkas, or pubs, or pizzas, and more got tossed into a crucible of race where European ethnicities got pulverized into whiteness. That whiteness is slapdash, pieced together from the European identities at hand. But there is a pattern to it all. It helped the steady climb of European cultures to dominance over the long haul of history.

Whiteness forged togetherness among groups in reverse, breaking down or, at least to a degree, breaking up ethnicity, and then building up an identity that was cut off from the old tongue and connected to the new land. So groups that were often at each other's throats learned to team up in the new world around whiteness. The battle to become American forced groups to cheat on their old selves and romance new selves. Old tribe for new tribe; old language for new language; old country for new one. The WASPs stung first, but the Italians landed plenty of blows, the Irish fought bare fisted, the Poles grimaced and bore in, and the Jews punched above their weight, all with one goal: to champion their arrival as Americans. That's how you went from being *just* Irish, *just* Italian, *just* Polish, or *just* Jewish to becoming white. So please don't deny this when you approach me to tell me about how your experience as a white ethnic parallels my experience as an African-American. The comparison ends at the hyphen.

My friends, I know reading this frightens many of you. It may even anger you. Please bear with me. Until you make whiteness give up its secrets none of us will get very far. Whiteness has privilege and power connected to it, no matter how poor you are. Of course the paradox is that even though whiteness is not real it is still true. I mean true as a force to be reckoned with. It is true because it has the power to make us believe it is real and to punish those who doubt its magic. Whiteness is slick and endlessly inventive. It is most effective when it makes itself invisible, when it appears neutral, human, American.

⁜   ⁜   ⁜

Let me share with you one of the first times I faced this truth as an adult. Last year I returned to Carson-Newman College, my alma mater, for the first time in thirty years. I had bolted from this southern Baptist outpost in Jefferson City, Tennessee—a dreadful throwback to Jim Crow—in 1985 after graduating with high honors and the top prize in philosophy. I had transferred there after spending two years at Knoxville College, a black school thirty miles up the highway that didn't have enough philosophy courses for my degree.

When I walked onto campus I got mugged by a version of whiteness that seemed to leap straight from a segregated bus in the fifties. Nestled within tree-lined streets, Carson-Newman still has a Mayberry feel all these years later, though Jefferson City isn't fictional, except in the way that all such towns spring from an innocent white imagination.

I hadn't been back since the president barred me from campus. It's not as if I got an official letter; there was no formal edict. But my failure to garner an invitation to return to school even after I gained notice in my vocation was proof enough. When I was a senior, the administration chose six students to make a commercial that would air in the region to promote the college. We had all received fellowships to attend prestigious graduate schools. Mine was the only one in the Ivy League.

The president wasted no time in summoning me to his office. Although the man had no doctorate, he still belonged to a fading southern aristocracy. He demanded that I produce proof on the spot that I'd gotten into Princeton. After all, Carson-Newman's name was on the line. If I turned out to be a fraud I could damage the college's reputation. I whipped out my offer letter from Princeton. He wasn't pleased, but neither was he deterred.

I was especially nervous because I owed the school seven thousand dollars in unpaid tuition. Sneering, the president looked me straight in the eyes and told me that I should get a job and pay my bill instead of going to Princeton. Until I did, my final transcript would be withheld. I quietly seethed.

A Princeton dean later assured me that the school had seen most of my grades and didn't require the transcript for me to enroll. But at the moment I had no such consolation. All I knew was that I'd made it through the blazing guns and bare-knuckled fists of Detroit and this white man wasn't going to stop me from getting to the Ivy League. I was desperate and determined. I wanted to tell the president that my straight A's in philosophy should have brought me more financial aid. But I was in no mood for begging. The moment of truth had arrived, and I was consumed by anger. I was angry that he had slung his invincible whiteness in my face. That anger turned to ice-cold rage and chilling verbal ire. If Ralph Ellison warned against doing brain surgery with a switchblade, I wasn't in much better shape, attempting heart surgery on my college president with a verbal safety pin, operating on him prick by prick.

"Sir, you must know that for me to take a job and give up a world-class education would be extremely shortsighted," I said frostily. "You've got to know the value of such a degree. But then, I suppose you have no way of knowing since you never earned a PhD."

He blushed beet red, sensing my contempt.

My defiance didn't defeat whiteness, but I took pride in giving it a body blow that day. I left his office, and shortly thereafter, the college, never to return, or to be invited back, until he was long gone. Some of my former professors confirmed that as soon as I left the college he heartily embraced the idea that I shouldn't come back. This was whiteness that demanded total deference to its will and way, a whiteness that demanded respect while offering none in return. The president was angry that I wouldn't let him ruin my life. He certainly tried.

Here's something else I learned in the company of white folk: my teachers and fellow students never had to say they were white until someone who wasn't white showed up. The

white people at my college saw me as a trespasser. But I
made them see that the whiteness they invested in wasn't
natural. It was, instead, a contrivance, a historical sleight
of hand. They swore that their invented history was objective and built on fact. Any other interpretation had to be
challenged. Whiteness has only two modes: it either converts or destroys. My black body was a thorn in the flesh of
whiteness. My very presence as a black man revealed that
whiteness was as artificial as the idea of race on which it
rested. And so my flesh, my history, my culture, my mind,
my tongue, my being had to be removed.

✢　✢　✢

I realize this is a lot for you to take in. It must make you
woozy and weak at the knees. So much has been invested
in whiteness that it is hard to let it go. It is often defensive,
resentful, full of denial and amnesia. The only way to save
our nation, and, yes, to save yourselves, is to let go of whiteness and the vision of American history it supports.

I'm not asking you to let go of your humanity, but, in
the best way possible, to find your way back to it. You can
let go of whiteness when you see it as a moral choice, an
ideology, a politic, a terribly fearful reaction to the thing it
hates the most but can least afford to do without: the black
people it helped to will into existence. White or black identity is nothing without the people and forces that make it
true. White and black folk are bound together, even when
we breathe very different meanings into race.

✢   ✢   ✢

My friends, when you have to confront identities or experiences that don't fit your view of the world, you fall back on preconceived notions that are no more real than the whiteness I've described. I learned this lesson even before my fateful meeting with the president of Carson-Newman.

One day his raven-haired assistant, with whom I'd formed a bond, delivered some troubling news.

"The administration thinks you're going to do something violent at graduation," the perky middle-aged white woman told me in a hastily called meeting in her office. After I assured her that I intended nothing of the sort, I stumbled out of her door, speechless.

I knew the president had sent her because he thought she had figured out the mystery of my blackness. I was sure she bragged about it, too, playing both ends against the middle. I didn't mind as long as the result was peace. But this was beyond the pale.

It was clear that I was as much a creation of their imaginations as whiteness itself. They may have been watching too many reruns of Blaxploitation films. This was only a decade after the era of *Shaft* and *The Mack* after all. Maybe they envisioned me out to get revenge against the white man like Pam Grier's characters in *Coffy* or *Foxy Brown*. Maybe they fantasized that I'd been reading Julius Lester's book *Look Out, Whitey! Black Power's Gon' Get Your Mama!* But "whitey" didn't have to worry about this child of Negroes. Hell, even some of their mamas thought I was cute and likable and invited me to dinner. True enough, I was more in the civil rights tradition than an advocate of black power, but I knew that it was all the same to most white folk. And I damn sure didn't sport any bell-bottoms or modish side-burns. I must confess, however, that I did constantly listen to Isaac Hayes' epic soundtrack to *Shaft,* so I may have con-fused the poor folk. No matter what, I came to understand Ralph Ellison's meaning when his unnamed character says, in the fourth line of *Invisible Man,* "I am invisible, under-stand, simply because people refuse to see me."

Carson-Newman upped the ante on Ellison. They not only tried to make me invisible, but they symbolically snatched my body and emptied out the contents of my black identity. In my absence they projected a woolly-haired phantom out to do them in. I couldn't possibly compete with this smaller-than-life stereotype. I was an ordained Baptist minister who had worked in a factory. I had a wife and child to take care of, and an education to get. I had no time for tomfoolery or terror. I had never as much as hinted that rage might flood my body. I had never participated in a formal protest, never written a letter to the editor of the col-lege newspaper. I had never expressed disgust at one racial problem or the next. I had never even raised my fist or voice.

I wasn't naïve. I knew that honest dialogue might rattle a white world that was not used to hearing a black man like me speak directly about race. No, my crime was far more mundane. I had whispered a prayer into a microphone in chapel during a Black History Month service asking God to help defeat racism in our midst. My few words set the white community on edge. My prayer was the clue that I wasn't mesmerized by the fictions of whiteness, that I wasn't satisfied with the sanctuary it wanted to provide. It was enough to tip off the president that I was ready for the Revolution and that I was prepared to bring it on violently. No other explanation made any sense.

✢ ✢ ✢

One thing you must understand, beloved, is that whiteness isn't a solo act. It's got a supporting cast. Lots of other things got created to uphold and justify whiteness. None was more seductive or necessary than the idea of American history. It may be hard for many of you to concede this. You think of history as a realm of complete objectivity. You think there are such things as indisputable facts, and those facts are woven together by neutral observers in a compelling story that is told as history. You think historians belong to a guild of chroniclers whose work is separate from what the culture considers important. You think they abide by the line from the sixties television series *Dragnet,* whose star character, the police sergeant Joe Friday, says famously, and dryly, "All we want are the facts, ma'am."

But the truth is that what so often passes for American history is really a record of white priorities or conquests set down as white achievement. That version of American history is a sprawling, bewildering chronicle, relentlessly revised. It ignores or downplays a variety of peoples, cultures, religions, and regions, all to show that history is as objective and as curious and as expansive as the white imagination allows. Of course, the notion that someone invents history is also to insist that everybody can, or does—though, it must be noted, not to equal effect.

I'm not arguing that most of you are delusional, or that facts of accomplishment and records of deeds don't exist. The delusion is whiteness itself.

In the end, history is never just what the people who experience it say it is. That's particularly true if those people are not in power, or if their voices, or their view of things, run counter to what the larger culture thinks is true—in short, what the larger culture thinks is valuable, justifiable, even righteous. The winners, alas, still write history. To say this out loud, in this day and age, when whiteness has congratulated itself for its tolerance of other cultures and peoples, is to invite real resistance from white America.

My dear friends, please try to understand that whiteness is limitless possibility. It is universal and invisible. That's why many of you are offended by any reference to race. You believe you are acting and thinking neutrally, objectively, without preference for one group or the next, including your own. You see yourselves as colorless until black folk dump the garbage of race on your heads. At your best moments you may concede that you started the race game, but you swear to the God you love that it is we black folk who keep it going. You have no idea how absurd that notion is, and yet we have grown accustomed to your defiance of common sense.

I got a taste of this when I taught at the University of North Carolina in the mid-nineties. I touched a raw nerve of race, and certainly whiteness, when I delivered a commencement address at the school in 1996. I knew that my speech might cause some controversy. There was no way that I could step to that podium and not offend the south's codes of polite bigotry just by speaking openly about the racial situation at hand. And even though whiteness had metastasized all over the country, its diseased core remained in the south, where black folk were fighting for their rightful place in society. But nonetheless I eagerly stepped into the Dean E. Smith stadium, where six thousand folk had gathered to wish their loved ones a joyous transition to another part of the real world.

(It irks me as a professor to hear folk describe the university as somehow unreal. It may be gilded, or privileged, certainly shielded, but it is no less real than, say, the corporate world, or sports, or the assembly line. We have real conversations, real conflicts, real thoughts, and real bodies to think those thoughts with.)

I grappled in my speech with whether America was still the dream that Martin Luther King, Jr., said it was in a commencement speech he delivered at Lincoln University 35 years earlier. King's audience was predominantly black, mine mostly white. In his 1961 speech "The American Dream," King said that "America is essentially a dream, a dream as yet unfulfilled." Two years later at the Lincoln Memorial King famously shared his dream with the nation. Four years after that, King declared that his dream had turned into a nightmare of church bombings, ghetto poverty, riots, and war.

I battled the notion that young folk were dragging the American dream down with their destructive pop culture and their social narcissism. I defended youth culture and wrestled with some of its most popular figures, from Kurt Cobain and Alanis Morissette to Snoop Dogg and Jenny McCarthy. I quoted the lyrics of The Notorious B.I.G. to make my point, including his use of the word "fuck," though, on reflection, I should have left it out. I didn't seek to offend the white grandparents and other kin who had gathered.

I defended affirmative action at graduation. Lawmakers had abolished it in California with the passage in 1996 of Proposition 209. That effort was led, painfully enough, by the University of California's regent, Ward Connerly, a conservative black man I'd soon debate. I deemed it my duty to use whatever platform I had to speak back to him. I also encouraged young white folk to appreciate the sacrifices made by some of their poor and less educated kin. Michael Jordan, the most famous alum of UNC, had recently given one million dollars to the university. Jordan said he didn't give it to the Black Cultural Center, though his mother then sat on the board, because the money would have been limited to one group. Instead he gave it to the School of Social Work, where, he said, the sum would benefit everyone. But the school of social work wasn't the law school, nor the school of dentistry, nor any other school in the university, and thus, the money couldn't possibly be for everyone. What saddened me about Jordan's comments was that even this black athletic legend believed that whiteness signified the universal. Blackness in his view signified the limited and particular. I challenged the black students to do better than Jordan and remember to help other blacks attain the American dream too.

There was no social media back then, but the local news-
papers lit me up. One called my speech "a political screed
dressed up in trendy academic gobbledygook." I suppose it's
racial progress of a sort when the black guy is accused of
speaking over the heads of white folk. An editorial cartoon
featured me sitting on a commode using toilet paper to prepare my next speech. There were calls for the university to
fire me, and a flurry of angry columns and letters to the editor. "He is not worth our tax money," one letter said.

But the real anger rang out from a sense of aggrieved
whiteness. One writer asked if the Constitution "protect[s]
black citizens but not white citizens?" Another writer
puzzled over the liberal discomfort with my speech since
progressives had "labored for years to disabuse us of any
notions of Western cultural superiority." He defended the
superiority of whiteness through a straw man argument
in the form of an extended conditional statement: "But if
America is not more than Africa, if Christmas is not more
than Kwanzaa, if William Shakespeare is not more than
Maya Angelou, then Dyson is not less than Demosthenes."
Then the kicker: "Chapel Hill, welcome to the Third
World." Whiteness had been challenged at its intellectual
and institutional heart.

Thankfully a few folk did defend me in public. One
letter argued that the paper's attempt "to discredit [Dyson]
by depicting [him] researching cultural expression in a lava-
tory" means the editorial staff "would benefit from attendance at one of Dyson's courses," since the attempt to place
"such expression in the context of the political economy and
cultural norms that dominate U.S. society, is profoundly

important." A fellow faculty member said that "this is an event when we shouldn't be afraid of words. Control emotions and try to listen to the message."

I must say that I was taken aback by the vitriol. The calls for me to be fired were one thing; but the scorn, even the death threats that came simply because I expressed a different view, a black view, were way over the top.

My friends, it's not as if I had only focused on reactionary white folk. As one letter said of my speech: "Rarely in one sitting can an individual insult Michael Jordan, white liberals, the black middle class, the United States and his own employers." My God, at least give me credit for being an equal opportunity offender! But white folk who get upset at being challenged hardly ever see the balance, never hear that they're not the only ones being singled out, even if one has just cause to indict whiteness to start with. I wasn't angry as much as I was saddened by the unvarnished hate and denial of reality that still pulsed in whiteness. But I should not have been surprised. After all, the country had just weathered a major racial catastrophe that revealed how blind whiteness could be.

✛   ✛   ✛

You must remember, beloved, that this was a year after O.J. Simpson had been acquitted of murdering his ex-wife Nicole Brown Simpson and her friend Ron Goldman. Race relations between black and white folk were tense. The Simpson acquittal was a "racequake" that revealed the fault lines that stretched beneath our national life. O.J.'s trial came on the heels of a tragic acquittal of four white policemen in 1992 for the savage beating in 1991 of Los Angeles motorist Rodney King. Black folk felt that they couldn't get a fair hearing in America's courts even when there was visual evidence of lethal whiteness. This may be read as an instance of dueling judgments: the not guilty Simpson verdict answered the not guilty verdict for the white officers. But the stakes were even higher. The King verdict, as it is known—funny how it is called that when it was the white cops being tried, suggesting that blackness is always on trial, always the object of dispute—was answered by a violent urban rebellion. More than 11,000 people were arrested, more than 2,000 were injured, and 55 people died.

The King and Simpson verdicts left America emotionally raw and at a brutal racial impasse. White folk got a rare chance to experience the sense of absurdity that black folk routinely feel when a clear case of injustice doesn't get resolved in court. Many of you were outraged and shocked that Simpson could get away with murder. A lot of you were miffed, even heartbroken, that black folk cheered Simpson's acquittal like it was Christmas in October. But you must see that the bitter taste left in your mouths was but a small taste of what black folk have swallowed from our first moments in this nation.

Maybe enough time has passed for us to admit that the Simpson verdict made liars of white and black folk alike.

But the lie began long before the Simpson trial. It has roots in whiteness itself, in whiteness that is a construct, an invention, that keeps white folk ignorant of black life. It makes so many of you, if we're honest, largely indifferent to black life. Admit it: you go on your merry white way as if the police aren't routinely hammering black folk without cause, aren't daily brutalizing us in front of your faces, aren't murdering black folk without so much as blinking an eye. You didn't care then. And tell the truth—many of you don't really care now.

Beloved, it's true that some of you are ashamed and embarrassed, but that is hardly enough. It looks bad to the rest of the world for all this havoc to be going on in America. It's not that the world loves us so much; it's that they feel you ought to be ashamed of yourselves for treating us this way. Now, I'm old enough to not be too fussy about how change comes about. What starts as shame may end as transformation. But even that can't be depended on. Whiteness grows more shameless, more cruel, more uncaring by the day. How many of you have really tried to put yourself in our position? It's hard to be white and empathetic to others. That sounds harsh, but that's a lesson that whiteness has taught its victims. Many of you were stuck, in 1995, and, sadly, even now, in a whiteness that didn't have to know, that wasn't punished for not knowing. It is hard for you to give up this willful ignorance. It is a drug. It is privilege and addiction. Your whiteness is a shield that keeps you from knowing what black folk must always know. Not until the Simpson verdict did many of you claim that you were finally awakened to what black folk had to know every day. But if so, you went back to sleep pretty damn quickly.

The Simpson verdict made black folk lie too. I'm not just telling you this now, my friends. I said it then to O.J.'s impossibly beautiful lawyer Johnnie Cochran. I know a lot of you hated him because he beat you at your own game. He sold his vision of history as the one that made the most sense to the group of people, his group of people, on that jury, whose decision, for once, mattered most. That's usually how whiteness operates in a nutshell. But this time, for a glancing moment, whiteness got coopted by a devilishly handsome chocolate barrister whose smooth words and hypnotic cadence left the jury and nation spellbound. I gave Cochran my full two cents when I ran into him after a weird and distressing phone call.

"Hello," I said as I took the phone from my wife.

"Should I call you reverend, or professor, or Dr. Dyson?" the familiar voice asked me. I nearly swallowed my spit. It was O.J.

I had just appeared that morning with infamous O.J. hater Geraldo Rivera on a national television show observing the fifth anniversary of the murders of Nicole and Ron. I had minced no words. I said that before the verdict there had been nothing black on Simpson but the bottom of his shoes. I also said that when O.J. took that long, slow ride down the L.A. freeway in A.C. Cowlings' iconic Bronco it wasn't the first time he used a white vehicle to escape a black reality. My words bit me in the butt that evening.

"You can call me Mike," I said in a voice that was an octave or two higher than my normal baritone register. Okay, the truth is I sounded like Mickey Mouse. O.J. had me scared and nearly speechless. My wife was in tears laughing at me.

"Speak like the courageous critic you're supposed to be," she teased me.

I gave her the "cut it out" gesture with my free hand slicing the air around my throat. She only laughed harder. It tickled her that I was squirming.

"I just want to clarify some things for you, Mr. Dyson," Simpson continued.

Simpson proceeded to relitigate the case. On and on he went for nearly 45 minutes. He even offered to come to my class at Columbia University and present his side of things. That made me especially nervous. He had one more thing to tell me.

"Geraldo said I only date blondes," O.J. said to me. "That's not true."

There was a beat. After the pause came his follow-up. It was vintage Simpson.

"I date redheads, brunettes, all types of women."

I didn't have the heart, really the courage, to say to him that wasn't Rivera's point. I didn't say to him that blonde hair was a synecdoche for the string of white women he dated, one of whom he married.

"Thank you for calling, Mr. Simpson," I said, hanging up the phone in shock, even as my wife's guffaws drowned out my thoughts.

A few days later I saw Johnnie Cochran.

"Hey man, why in the hell did you give O.J. my number?" I asked in only half-feigned outrage. I knew that Johnnie was the only way his most famous client got those digits.

"Professor, he just wanted to speak to you," Cochran said as he flashed that million-dollar smile of his.

"He had me shook," I told Johnnie, lapsing into black vernacular. "I know he kill white people, but do he kill black people too? I know you his lawyer, and you can't say nothing, man, but you know he killed them people."

Cochran just laughed.

I didn't take any surveys, but I believed that most black folk knew deep in our hearts that O.J. Simpson murdered Nicole and Ron. There's more evidence against O.J. than there is for the existence of God. It's not that Marcia Clark and her team didn't do their due diligence. O.J.'s accusers and prosecutors lost before they stepped into the court. The hurts and traumas against black folk had piled so high, the pain had resonated so deeply, and the refusal of whiteness to open its eyes had become so abhorrent that black folk sent a message to white America. No amount of evidence against Simpson could possibly match the far greater evidence of racial injustice against black folk. And you can't claim ignorance here, my friends. If a videotape recording of a black man going down under the withering attack of four white police couldn't convince you of the evil of your system, then nothing could.

The celebration of the not guilty verdict was a big "fuck you" from black America. It was the politest way possible to send a message you had repeatedly, tragically, willfully ignored: things are not okay in the racial heartland. Black folk weren't necessarily aware that they were doing this. Here blackness operated like whiteness does. The black perception of what was convincing, or not, was shaped by jurors' experiences. It was molded by the black community's heartbreak. It seemed to black folk that the only way to combat white privilege was with the exercise of a little black privilege.

And even though the egregious errors of the criminal justice system existed long before Simpson, the constant refusal ever since to even charge most white police in the killing of unarmed black motorists is a kind of collective payback for O.J.

Can't you see, my friends, that whiteness is determined to get the last word? That it is determined once again to make its unspoken allegiances and silent privilege the basis of justice in America? Don't you see it's your way or no way at all? Please don't pretend you don't understand us. You didn't get mad when all of those white folk who killed black folk got away with murder in the sixties. Byron De La Beckwith bragged for years about killing Medgar Evers in 1963. He was finally convicted in 1994. The men who killed Emmett Till got off scot-free, even though everybody knew they lynched that poor child. That's ancient history to you. But that history got a hearing in the Simpson verdict: Medgar; the three civil rights workers murdered in Mississippi; the four girls bombed in the Birmingham church; poor 15-year-old Latasha Harlins, who was brutally shot down in a store in Los Angeles in 1991; and every instance of police brutality unanswered by the state, every unjustified killing of black flesh. The Simpson verdict was your forced atonement.

O.J. awakened your collective white rage. That or you're obsessed with him because he's the one that got away, the one who challenged your view of whiteness, made you madder than anybody—that is, until Obama. But there's little real justification for Obama hate, except that he was a black man in charge of our country, and many whites wanted to take it back and make it great again. Hence, the election of Donald Trump as president.

And let's be real: O.J.'s betrayal hurt worse than Obama's ascent. O.J. shared your worldview. O.J. took full advantage of the privilege you offered him as an honorary white man. He accepted the bargain in a way Obama never did, never could. Your anger for O.J. is that he was, finally—like you fear all black folk could potentially be—an ungrateful *nigger*. O.J. seemed to fully revel in whiteness and gladly deny that he was black, that is, until he got in trouble. Then that racial reflex kicked in: back against the wall, black against the wall.

You shouldn't be too angry with O.J. He's as white a black man as there's been in the last half century. Even Clarence Thomas is blacker than O.J. It is true that Thomas is a darker version of Simpson. But Thomas was reviled by black culture for his dark skin. He repays us with decisions on the Supreme Court that mock our humanity and lower his dignity with each stroke of his pen.

What the Simpson case makes clear is that even though whiteness is an invention, it is nontransferable, at least to black folk. No matter how we try we still can't be white, can't truly enjoy white privilege. Many of you were willing to chalk up the black belief in Simpson's innocence—well, truly, black folk never claimed Simpson was innocent, just not guilty, a distinction that whiteness has taught us—as an instance of black denial, of black delusion. It never occurred to you that that is just how whiteness operates at all times. It's been that way ever since it was created a few centuries back to justify treating black people like dogs. It has stayed that way right up until this moment.

✠ ✠ ✠

I must say to you, my friends, that teaching in your schools has shown me that being white means never having to say you're white. Whiteness long ago, at least in America, shed its ethnic skin and struck a universal pose. Whiteness never had to announce its whiteness, never had to promote or celebrate its unique features.

If whites are history, and history is white, then so are culture, and society, and law, and government, and politics; so are logic and thinking and reflection and truth and circumstances and the world and reality and morality and all that means anything at all.

Yes, my friends, your hunger for history is still pretty segregated. Your knowledge of America often ends at the color line. You end up erasing the black story as the American story, black history as American history.

You certainly have an insatiable thirst for history, but only if that history justifies whiteness. Most black folk can't help but notice what many whites rarely wish, or are compelled, to see: you embrace history as your faithful flame when she kisses you, and yet you spurn her as a cheating mate when she nods or winks at others. You love history when it's yet another book about, say, the Founding Fathers. No amount of minutia is too tedious. No new fact is too obscure to report. The curiosity about presidents is nearly inexhaustible.

History is a friend to white America when it celebrates the glories of American exceptionalism, the beauty of American invention, the genius of the American soul. History is unrestrained bliss when it sings Walt Whitman's body electric or touts the lyrical vision of the Transcendentalists. History that swings at the plate with Babe Ruth or slides into home with Joe DiMaggio is the American pastime at its best. History hovers low in solemn regard for the men who gave up the ghost at Appomattox and speaks with quiet reverence for the Confederate flags that gleefully waved to secession. Of course all of you don't sing from the same hymnal. But American history, the collective force of white identity that picks up velocity across the centuries, mouths every note.

Beloved, I must admit that I've encountered many of you as white allies who know that whiteness is privilege and power. You know that white skin is magic, that it is a key to open doors. Yet you also know that whiteness for the most part remains invisible to many white folk.

It has been striking, too, to observe whites for whom their whiteness isn't a passport to riches, whites for whom whiteness offers no material reward. But there is a psychological and social advantage in not being thought of as black; poor whites seem to say, "At least there's a nigger beneath me." And it's a way for poor whites to be of value to richer whites, especially when poor whites agree that black folk are the source of their trouble—not the corporate behavior of wealthier whites who hurt black and white folk alike. It's a way to bond beyond class. It's a way for working class whites to experience momentary prestige in the eyes of richer whites. And there are a lot of privileges that white folk get that don't depend on cash. The greatest one may be getting stopped by a cop and living to talk about it.

✣   ✣   ✣

After more than a century of enlightened study we know that race is not just something that falls from the sky; it is, as the anthropologists say, a fabricated idea. But that doesn't mean that race doesn't have material consequence and empirical weight. It simply means that if we constructed it, we can get about the business of deconstructing it.

And there is a paradox that many of you refuse to see: to get to a point where race won't make a difference, we have to wrestle, first, with the difference that race makes. The idea that whiteness should be abolished, an idea that some white antiracist thinkers have put forth, disturbs a lot of you—especially when you argue that whiteness is not all murder and mayhem. Historian David Roediger has questioned if there is a "white culture outside of domination." At the University of Minnesota, where he taught for five years, conservative white kids on campus said there was a need for a white cultural center if a black cultural center existed. When he asked his class what they'd put in a white cultural center, he said "there was the longest silence that I have ever experienced in a classroom." The silence "was broken by a hand going up, and a shout: 'Elvis!' And then laughter, that Elvis would somehow be considered unambiguously white." Of course there was laughter. If ever there's been what Norman Mailer termed a white Negro, at least in style, and one who's made money and his reputation off a derivative blackness, it's Elvis Presley. If Elvis belongs in a white cultural center, then so do Chuck Berry and Little Richard.

Beloved, I haven't given up on your ability to confront whiteness, to give it the old college try, literally. Back at my alma mater Carson-Newman, after being banned for 31 years, and even though I felt the time warp, I also got cause for hope. When I preached in the chapel, I was certainly far more blunt and vocal in challenging whiteness than I had been when I went to school there. I preached about the black prophetic mission and its demand for social change. I riled up some conservative white students. Many got up and walked out. To paraphrase Yogi Berra, it was racial déjà vu all over again.

But I also spoke of the need to combat class inequality, gender oppression, and homophobia. I tried to link these ills and thus lighten the load of responsibility that white folk would have to carry alone. But those young conservatives still got mad. I suspected they hadn't heard a sermon like mine before, hadn't had to hear it, either, at least not in the school's chapel or their home churches. Some of the students threatened to protest my presentation later that evening where the entire local community gathered. I told the folk in charge that I didn't mind that at all, and that I'd be more than happy to entertain their questions and to answer their outrage.

The protest never happened. But one of the angriest young men stayed behind to ask me a question as I signed copies of my books. He wanted to know how I could be a Christian and say the things I do; that I should take into account views with which I disagreed. I assured him that doubting my Christianity put him in good stead with many black folk I know, who, because of my stand against homophobia, count me among the religiously unwashed. Let me be real: my joyful embrace of the secular dimensions of black culture has landed me in trouble. It makes a lot of folk uncomfortable when I taunt the supposed abyss between the sacred and profane. I told the young man that to be black in America means always taking in views we disagree with, not out of altruism, but out of necessity and the impulse to survive. I gently insisted that he take off the blinders to his whiteness. I encouraged him to think of how he was reared and what role that had on his views, and how his rearing had a lot to do with the privileges of whiteness. I knew my crash course in whiteness wouldn't convince him. But at least he listened. Instead of an angry protest, we shared an open, honest conversation. I asked him to recall an earlier question from one of his classmates in the audience, in whose voice I detected a fellow traveler.

"For a white working class kid, who learned about Western philosophy from reading the sermons and speeches and essays of Dr. King—that was actually how I learned about old dead white people, is through a black man. Given that context, how would somebody in my position be an ally? How . . . do I seek to supplant imperialism, how do I seek to supplant militarism, how do I seek to supplant white supremacy and the patriarchy without perpetuating those very same things through my action?"

Answering this earnest young man, I acknowledged the limitations of our subject positions. I also acknowledged that our lives are constantly in process. I told him that some of the greatest victims of whiteness are whites themselves, having to bear the burden of a false belief in superiority. I told him how I also loved the words of many old dead white men, from Tennyson to Merle Haggard, even though many of those white men would find me troublesome. I asked him not only to challenge white privilege, but also to resist the narcissism that celebrates one's challenge to whiteness rather than siding with those who are its steady victims. Working as a white ally is tough, but certainly not impossible. Learning to listen is a virtue that whiteness has often avoided. I asked him to engage, to adopt the vocabulary of empathy, to develop fluidity in the dialect of hope and the language of racial understanding.

It felt at that moment, on that night, that something good might happen. I had no reason to doubt that at many other moments like this, on many other similar nights, hope might prevail. If you, my friends, would make a conscious effort to change. If you would stop being white.

2.

THE FIVE STAGES OF WHITE GRIEF

Let's face it, you've grieved ever since you were forced to share some of your historical shine with the black folk you'd kept underfoot for centuries. You didn't think we deserved that much attention; you've tried to hide us, even bury us, for too long. First we were the enslaved lackeys at your beck and call, then the servants at the family dinner. Later we were the embarrassing kinfolk at the family picnic. We finally made it to the holiday gathering too, but your paternalism relegated us to the children's table. You were forced to invite us to affairs of state, but you mostly ignored us.

It has been exceedingly tough for you to wrap your minds around the notion that black folk are your equals in any realm. The exception might be sports, but you control the purse strings there, too, so no sweat off your billions. And as long as we know our place, and don't, for instance, take a knee while the national anthem is played to protest injustice, we are well rewarded for our athletic exploits—gladiators for your titillation and fantasy leagues. But when that fantasy is up, and proper black manhood and womanhood is reclaimed, we know that you revert to your old ways and think of us as not worth the trouble. In most other realms of pursuit you deem us largely incompetent and ir-relevant, and yet black folk, and the rest of the rainbow of colors too, keep proving you wrong.

It is being proved wrong that leaves you distressed. There is often sorrow and anguish in white America when blackness comes in the room. It gives you a bad case of what can only be called, colloquially, the racial blues, but more formally, let's name it C.H.E.A.T. (Chronic Historical Evasion and Trickery) disorder. This malady is characterized by bouts of depression when you can no longer avoid the history that you think doesn't matter much, or when your attempts to deceive yourself and others—about the low quality of all that isn't white—fall flat. It's understandable that you experience mood swings. It bears some resemblance to the five stages of grief a person passes through when they know they're dying.

You're determined not to lose the battle to control the historical narrative. After all, you realize that the pressure to broaden the scope of American history pries loose your head-lock on the national mythology. Other cultures and other peoples are having their say as well, especially the black voices that have too long been suppressed. So you portray black-ness as the enemy of all that is smart, or sophisticated, or uplifting, or worth emulating or transmitting. But the debt American culture owes to black folk can't be easily erased, so you fight even harder to keep our story from being told in all its unforgiving brilliance and its undiscouraged beauty.

Yet you don't seem ever, finally, to win the war to keep our history hidden. And the more you lose that battle, mostly because it's built on lies, the more you kick your defensiveness into higher gears and vent your frustration, resentment, and sadness. So the quicker you admit you're a (victim of) C.H.E.A.T., that you've got it bad and that ain't good, the better off you will be, and the rest of us will be too. If not treated early on, C.H.E.A.T. leads to other disorders, including F.A.K.E. (Finding Alternative Knowledge Elusive), F.O.O.L. (Forsaking Others' Outstanding Literacy), and L.I.E. (Lacking Introspection Entirely).

The only way for you to overcome C.H.E.A.T. is to confront the disorder head-on and acknowledge the five stages of white racial grief that you experience as you grapple with the presence of black folk and the history they created—and the very way they have changed American society. You are often stumped by feats of black competence; or you display a tolerance for blackness that slides quickly to condescension. There is resistance and rage too. There is anger at the refusal of the "other" to cave in to whiteness, to see history, American history, the way you see it, anger at our refusal to curtail black agency. During the eighties and nineties and the ballyhooed canon wars, you were fit to be tied when a writer like Toni Morrison, who should have been recognized long ago for her genius, finally got her due as an American master. It upsets you when black folk say that white history dressed up as American history is not a perfect picture of reality.

Beloved, white racial grief erupts when you fear losing your dominance. You get mighty angry at our demand that you live up to the sense of responsibility you say others should have—especially black folk and people of color. You often tell us to pull ourselves up by our bootstraps, to make no excuses for our failures, and to instead admit our flaws and better ourselves. And yet so many of you, beloved, are obstinate to a fault, intransigent and thin-skinned when it comes to accepting the calling out you effortlessly offer to others. Donald Trump is only the most recent and boisterous example.

The first stage of white racial grief is to plead utter ignorance about black life and culture. It seems impossible to pull off, but many of you appear to live in what the late writer and cultural critic Gore Vidal called "The United States of Amnesia." When black folk get in your face, or even just expect you to know a little about black life, to take the past into account when speaking about black life, your reaction is often, simply, to forget it. It is a willful refusal to know. So often many of you claim no knowledge of black life, as if it never played a role in your world or made a difference to your existence. But it is no less distressing that you can so easily dismiss the history of a people you share space and time with as you both carve out your destiny together on the same national geography. It is not unlike those explorers and pilgrims who "discovered" America, that is, discovered a land full of native people. Native lives stopped mattering before they ever began to count.

The historical erasure of blackness strengthens this racially blind version of American history, makes it easier to make the argument that black folk never did a damn thing for the nation. Iowa congressman Steve King wondered in 2016 where in history "are these contributions that have been made by these other categories of people . . . where did any other subgroup of people [other than whites] contribute more to civilization?" King said that Western civilization is "rooted in Western Europe, Eastern Europe and the United States of America and every place where the footprint of Christianity settled the world."

Let's be honest, my friends, this kind of sentiment is far more widespread than you may care to admit. It makes one thing clear: black and white folk are often speaking different languages with no common frame of reference, and therefore, no possibility of understanding each other. Thus the crudest conclusions possible in American history have stuck to black life. Black folk are often seen as simians at the high table of culture, aping white society. This poisons public discourse, distorting the history of American politics. Liberal professor Mark Lilla argued that Hillary Clinton's "calling out explicitly to African-American" and other groups in the 2016 campaign "was a strategic mistake" because it left out the white working class and the highly religious. But the history of American politics is the history of accommodating whiteness at many levels, and while religiously influenced working class folk surely need to be heeded, it is odd that Lilla's invective against identity politics appeals to the religiously rooted white working class at the expense of the black or brown religiously influenced working classes. Lilla's view is amnesia with a bang, or really, a fang, an exposed snarl at the inconvenient messiness of real history.

Real American history is the sticky web in which black and white are stuck together. Stop trying to pretend that you don't know this. You can kill us, even brutalize us, but history makes escape from us impossible. An even greater fear lurks barely beneath the surface. What horrifies many of you

is that America, at its root, has been in part made by blackness. God forbid, but it may in part be black. Slavery made
America a slave to black history. As much as white America
invented us, the nation can never be free of us now. America
doesn't even exist without us. That's why Barack Obama was
so offensive, so scary to white America. America shudders
and says to itself: The president's supposed to be *us,* not *them.*
In that light, Donald Trump's victory was hardly surprising.

The one-drop rule, the notion to racial purists that even
a speck of black blood contaminates one's heritage, has always signified that white America believed that blackness
was superior. Even the slightest presence of black blood was
able to overcome and outsmart whiteness. Blackness had to
be taboo because it couldn't be vanquished or destroyed.
Blackness feels like a curse to your view of history.

White America, you deliberately forget how whiteness caused black suffering. And it shows in the strangest
ways. You forget how you kept black folk poor as share-
croppers. You forget how you kept us out of your classrooms and in subpar schools. You forget how you denied
us jobs, and when we got them, how you denied us promo-
tions. You forget how you kept us out of the suburbs, and
now that you're gentrifying our inner city neighborhoods,
you're pushing us to the suburbs. You forget that you kept
us from voting, and then blamed us for being lackadaisical
at the polls. Although it sounds delusional, perhaps more
than a few of you feel the way Donald Trump's former
campaign chair in Mahoning County, Ohio, Kathy Miller,
does. "If you're black and you haven't been successful in
the last 50 years, it's your own fault," Miller said. "You've

had every opportunity, it was given to you. You've had the same schools everybody else went to. You had benefits to go to college that white kids didn't have. You had all the advantages and didn't take advantage of it. It's not our fault, certainly." She also said, "I don't think there was any racism until Obama got elected."

Think of how the members of the House of Representatives, influenced by the Tea Party, opened the 112th Congress in 2011 by reading out loud on the House floor the Constitution in its entirety. Except they didn't read the entire, or the original, version, which included Article 1, Section 2, which says that black folk equaled three-fifths of a white person. The representatives lapsed into calculated forgetting.

That sort of behavior is not limited to the mostly white men who make up our Congress. It bleeds into the general population as well. How many high school social studies textbooks, like the one prepared for use in Texas, forget racial terror by downplaying slavery and barely mentioning segregation, presenting a seamless transition from bondage to freedom?

Toni Morrison, in her great novel *Beloved,* replaces memory and forgetting with "rememory" and "disremember" to help us think about who, or what, the nation chooses to remember or forget. President Donald Trump chose "Make America Great Again" as his 2016 campaign slogan. It sounded the call to white America to return to simpler, better days. But the golden age of the past is a fiction, a projection of nostalgia that selects what is most comforting to remember. It summons a past that was not great for all; in fact, it is a past that was not great at all, not with racism and sexism clouding the culture. Going back to a time that was great depends on deliberate disremembering.

One of the great perks of being white in America is the capacity to forget at will. The sort of amnesia that blankets white America is reflected in an Alan Bergman and Marilyn Bergman lyric sung by Barbra Streisand: "What's too painful to remember we simply choose to forget." The second stage of grief flashes in the assertion "it didn't happen." Instead of "forget it," there is "deny it." Civil rights icon Joseph Lowery often says that we live in the fifty-first state, the state of denial. Denial is even more sinister than amnesia because there is some concession to facts that are then roundly negated. Here is where the gaslight effect goes wild. Black folk are made to feel crazy for believing something they know to be true.

Beloved, you must admit that denial of fact, indeed denial as fact, has shaped your version of American history. This is how you can ingeniously deny your role in past racism. You acknowledge that bigotry exists. For instance, you will often say that separate but equal public policy was bad. You just don't find too many current examples of the persistence of racism, like the fact that, given they have the same years of education, a white man with a criminal record is often more likely to get a job than a black man with no record. Or that even when they commit the same crime, black folk are more likely to do more time than a comparable white person. Or that a black male born in 2001 has a 32 percent chance of going to jail—a one-in-three shot—whereas a Latino has a 17 percent chance, and a white male a 6 percent chance. Or that black women are far more likely than others to be evicted. Or that police stop black and brown folk far more than white folk. Or that black folk are frequently illegally excluded from jury service. Sure, there are no white and black water fountains, but inequality persists.

White denial thrives on shifts and pivots. "It was my ancestors, not me, who did this to you." But what looks like confession is really denial. The "them, not me" defense denies how the problem persists in the present day. It is best to think of systems and not individuals when it comes to racial benefit in white America. Thinking of it in individual terms removes blame from many of you who are present beneficiaries of past behavior. The institutions of national life favor your success, whether that means you get better schools and more jobs, or less punishment and less jail. Not because you're necessarily smarter, or better behaved, but because being white offers you benefits, understanding, and forgiveness where needed. A great deal of white advantage has nothing to do with how you actively resist black success, or the success of other people of color. It's what you do for each other, how you take each other into account, that makes up a lot of what we have come to call "white privilege."

When it comes to race the past is always present. What Jim Crow achieved in the past through, say, redlining—where services like banking, insurance, health care, and supermarkets are denied to specific racial or ethnic groups—continues to this day. Formal segregation in housing policies may have been struck down, but steering, where real estate brokers direct home buyers toward or away from particular neighborhoods based on race, is as effective as ever. School segregation is no longer the law of the land, but classrooms today are depressingly re-segregated.

Yet no one is responsible. All we hear is the refrain from reggae star Shaggy's hit, "It wasn't me." We end up with what social scientist Eduardo Bonilla-Silva calls "racism without racists."

My friends, if you simply look around, and reflect on even recent history, you'll see that denial shows up in painful ways, even among young folk. A recent study by the Public Religion Research Institute shows that 56 percent of Millennials think that the government spends too much on black and minority issues, and an even higher number think that white folk suffer discrimination, and it is just as big a problem as that suffered by black folk and other minorities. Or those white youth wonder why they don't have a White Entertainment Channel to match BET.

In the political realm, look at the Supreme Court in its *Shelby v. Holder* voting rights amendment decision. The Court struck down the requirement to get legal permission to change voting practices because it concluded such permission was no longer necessary. The court denied the primary reason for recent black voting success: the existence of the rule for preclearance—where a jurisdiction covered under the law cannot change voting procedure without written approval from the Department of Justice—in Section Four of the Voting Rights Act. Now they were throwing it out because the very success of the rule counted as evidence that it was no longer needed. It was a nifty and nasty bit of circular reasoning that denied the facts. Can you not imagine how this sort of reasoning makes us just a little bit crazy? How it makes us think that white folk are hell-bent on denying how much the past is still with us? Black folk were successfully voting because they were being protected. Supreme Court justice Ruth Bader Ginsburg torched her conservative colleagues with blistering eloquence. She argued that "throwing out preclearance [the Section Four formula] when it has worked and is continuing to work to stop discriminatory changes is like throwing away your umbrella because you are not getting wet." That's just one example of why Ginsburg may be black folks' favorite justice since the death of Thurgood Marshall—despite calling Colin Kaepernick's protest of police brutality "dumb and disrespectful," an issue I'll take up later.

Instances of denial clutter the landscape. Fox News channels such denial nightly. I'm distressed to see the right-wing network blaring from the television screens in the restaurants of hotels I stay in when I'm on the road in states like Ohio or Florida. Places where working class and poor whites don't fare so well, and yet they cling to the racial fantasies of going back to a time when they ran things. But just as it was true when, say, Ronald Reagan was in office, working class whites and their poor kin won't benefit from the economic policies of the conservative politicians they depend on to diss black people and other minorities. What they gain from not being seen as black they lose in real economic terms. It's a Faustian racial bargain.

The third stage of white racial grief, appropriation, looms everywhere. If black history can't be forgotten or denied, white America can, simply, take it. Appropriation is a tricky symptom of white racial grief, and one that, ironically, defers to black culture even as it displaces it. White culture bows at the shrine of black culture in order to rob it of its riches. White America loves black style when its face and form are white.

Rachel Dolezal, former president of the NAACP in Seattle, Washington, caused quite a stir when she lied about her racial identity, which was white, and claimed to be black. She was eventually forced to leave her post at the NAACP. Dolezal didn't feel that her white identity should in any way still the heart of blackness that beat within her. White Australian rapper Iggy Azalea mimicked the dialect of the hood in America to cash in on the desire to have white hip-hop stars equal the achievements of their black peers, much like the truly great Eminem. Eminem has paid homage to hip-hop culture with extraordinary talent and hard work, just as Justin Timberlake does with rhythm and blues, except, in the case of Timberlake, he picks and chooses his way through blackness. He's black at awards time, not so much when it comes to taking heat with Janet Jackson over their controversial halftime Super Bowl performance in which he tore off part of her clothing at the end of their act. Timberlake proves that cultural critic Greg Tate is right: such white stars want everything but the burden of the blackness they sample. The credo of appropriators is "it happened to me too." Blackness, that is, but not its costs or penalties. Moreover, these stars claim an outsider status without actually having to be outsiders.

The novelist Lionel Shriver threw an opening salvo in the newest installment of the writing wars to determine who could say what about whom. Shriver dropped her bomb in 2016 when she addressed the Brisbane Writers Festival and rode herd on her free speech horse against political correctness. Millennials, and the generation trailing them, are especially vulnerable on this score, Shriver argued, because they are in a race "to see who can be more righteous and aggrieved—who can replace the boring old civil rights generation with a spikier brand." As Shriver sees it, the left has become all too nervous about living in the skin or brain or experiences of the other. The demand that folk write only about what they know or experience is utter nonsense to Shriver; it is suffocating orthodoxy that imperils the art of the novel. "Otherwise, all I could write about would be smart-alecky 59-year-old 5-foot-2-inch white women from North Carolina." It's easy to empathize with Shriver; after all, if you only write what you know, then you are left with precious little to write about.

Shriver's argument, however, fails to see how other cultures—their people, their ideas, their identities—have always been treated as only fiction, have always been looted of their inherent value and forced to fit in to the schemes, worldviews, or novels of folk, especially white folk, who were invested in denying their own privilege and power to treat these other cultures just as they pleased. When Shriver talks about "free speech," she gets the speech part right; but she only sees "free" from the perspective of the person doing the writing, not the one being written about. Shriver as a white writer is quite free to roam across the globe in search of whatever experiences or insights will light her way to a nuanced, engaged piece of fiction.

But that freedom is not merely artistic; in fact, her art, the art of white writers, rests on power relations that have left black culture at a disadvantage, vulnerable to literary cherry-picking. Shriver's grumbling is dressed up as the will to free expression, which should characterize the art of writing in any truly liberated culture. But underneath her gripes are a body of ideas and identities that have been abused, and appropriated, against the will of other cultures, and used at the discretion of writers who pay no mind to the people whose experiences they seek to borrow. Those people of color, for instance, have been cogs in the cultural machinery of white writers. Of course the writers' purpose might be a good one, such as telling a story that hasn't been told. But if the folk whose story is told don't have the opportunity to tell their own story, what is on the surface a good thing becomes a matter of who has the power and privilege to spin narratives.

We must also not overlook how the use of such experiences can reinforce beliefs about communities of color that have harmful political consequences, such as William Styron's controversial novel *The Confessions of Nat Turner,* which painted Turner as a man more obsessed with violent sexual lust for a blonde teenager than political rebellion against slavery. Nor should we ignore how the appropriation of "minority" cultures by white writers with a political advantage leaves people of color little room to speak their truths in their own ways.

And we certainly can't ignore how the more famous members of your tribe often get angry when they're called on their appropriation. Fashion designer Marc Jacobs used candy-colored Etsy dreadlocks on mostly nonblack models in his 2016 fashion show, provoking ire and outrage. Critics claimed he trafficked in the worst sort of racial appropriation. Jacobs shot back at "all who cry 'cultural appropriation' or whatever nonsense about any race of skin color wearing their hair in a particular style or manner." Jacobs displayed great insensitivity and ignorance when he argued that it's "funny how you don't criticize women of color for straightening their hair." The reason for the lack of criticism may be simple: white folk have no corner on the straight-hair market, as witnessed by Asian and Latino follicles. Jacobs exposed his unconscious bias when he, of course, tried to claim the opposite: "I don't see color or race—I see people."

Too bad that so many white folk believe that pretending not to see race is the way to address racism, and that when they get caught seeing race *for* their advantage—as in using the natural hairstyles of black folk—they claim not to see race *to* their advantage. Jacobs overlooks the point that black folk wearing their hair in locks at work is often seen as inappropriate; dreadlocks are widely viewed as incompatible with our nation's business culture. Black folk can't choose to wear their hair in locks and get work, an option that only white folk appear capable of choosing. Basically Marc Jacobs wants us to shut up and not notice that he's ripping off black culture. He is inspired by us and pays homage to us—in a supposedly nonracial fashion—while he refuses to see color. You see how this can so quickly go south? How about just giving credit where credit is due?

The irony is that well-meaning white folk like Marc Jacobs draw their inspiration from a misreading of the civil rights movement and the example of Martin Luther King, Jr. The civil rights movement that inspired King, that he inspired in turn, has been appropriated too, and often in troubling ways. We end up with a greatly compromised view of the black freedom struggle. In the narrative of American history, especially the kind told in our nation's textbooks, the movement didn't seek racial justice as much as it sought a race-neutral society. American history hugs colorblindness. If you can't see race you certainly can't see racial responsibility. You can simply remain blind to your own advantages. When some of you say, "I don't see color," you are either well-intending naïfs or willful race evaders. In either case you don't help the cause. The failure to see color only benefits white America. A world without color is a world without racial debt.

One of the greatest privileges of whiteness is not to see color, not to see race, and not to pay a price for ignoring it, except, of course, when you're called on it. But even then, that price pales, quite literally, in comparison to the high price black folk pay for being black. We pay a price, too, for not even being able to derive recognition, and financial reward, for the styles that make the world want to be black so bad that they don't mind looking like us, as long as they never, ever have to be us.

If the appropriators can freely rip off our culture with no consequences, those who revise racial history—the fourth stage of white racial grief—are even less accountable for their deeds.

The way of the racial revisionist, when it comes to black life and history, is, simply, to rewrite it. Their motto is, "It didn't happen that way." There is a flood of writing that tells us that the Civil War wasn't really about slavery but about the effort to defend states' rights. But, my friends, you've got to put yourself in our place and see the absurdity of such a claim. Defend the right of the state to do what? To enslave blacks. But even here the irresistible logic of whiteness, that is, irresistible to whites themselves—and to all of us who are subject to white whim—springs into full action. White American history is so powerful that even when it loses it wins, at least in skirmishes within whiteness itself. From the right wing there is the belief that the Civil War was fought over the ability of individual states to beat back a federal government out to impose its will. From the left wing there's the belief that the Civil War was a conflict between the planter class and the proletariat. In each case, race as the main reason for the war is skillfully rewritten, or, really, written out.

Slavery is rewritten too. Some white Christian apologists contended that black folk needed slavery to save their souls, or to rescue their cultures. A contemporary twist on this argument radiates in thinkers like Dinesh D'Souza, who claims that American blacks brought here through slavery are now doing far better than their African kin. Some white critics argue that since blacks sold other blacks into slavery, bondage was a black man's problem, not a white man's burden. But revisionists would much rather describe the dehumanization of black folk as little more than a commercial transaction. It's another way of washing their hands of racial responsibility.

The effort to rewrite history surfaces in how Malcolm X is treated in the mainstream. It hardly seems likely that the culture he fought with all his heart could be depended on to grasp his true meaning. Malcolm is often read as an apostle of violence, as a frightful figure consumed by destructive rage. Yet the truth is far more complex; and Malcolm was far more complicated. But isn't *The Autobiography of Malcolm X* so enduringly appealing because it shows Malcolm X giving up on hatred as a means to racial justice? Malcolm X believed in the liberation of black folk from the mental and psychological chains of white supremacy. He was not committed to nonviolence as a way of life or a method of social strategy. He believed that such a commitment prevents the full realization of black emancipation. Yet he was not personally violent. As Ossie Davis said in his eulogy, responding to the claim that Malcolm preached hate and was a fanatic and a racist: "Did you even talk to Brother Malcolm? . . . Was he ever himself associated with violence or any public disturbance?" The rage that flowed in Malcolm's veins was the rage against a force of whiteness that aimed to wash its black kin from the face of the earth.

The urge to rewrite black history occasionally gives way to the final stage of white racial grief, which is, simply, when it comes to race, to dilute it. That is, to argue that bad stuff doesn't just plague black folk. To summarize: "Bad stuff happens to everyone." This argument surfaced in the aftermath of Hurricane Katrina. The storm certainly hit black folk, but it hit white folk too. This is the sordid version of reverse American exceptionalism.

It is the same "me too" impulse that flares in the bitter battle against affirmative action. Beloved, I can't help but notice that affirmative action is the bee in so many of your bonnets. You look around in your classrooms and you think every black person is there because they got an unfair shake from the system. You look at your job and you think that your black coworker got an unjust nod of approval from the powers that be.

You never stop to think how the history of whiteness in America is one long scroll of affirmative action. You never stop to think that Babe Ruth never had to play the greatest players of his generation—just the greatest white players. You never stop to think that most of our presidents never rose to the top because they bested the competition just the white competition. White privilege is a self-selecting tool that keeps you from having to compete with the best. The history of white folk gaining access to Harvard, Princeton, or Yale is the history of white folk deciding ahead of the game that you were superior. You argue that slots in school should be reserved for your kin, because, after all, they are smarter, more disciplined, better suited, and more deserving than inferior blacks.

That's like concluding that the Cleveland Cavaliers can't possibly win the NBA championship because they are down three-games-to-one to the Golden State Warriors. Throw in the towel and call it a series. But they must play the series to determine the winner. Whiteness is having all the advantages on your side—the referees blowing the whistle for you, the arena packed with only your fans. In fact, whiteness means you never even have to play the game at all, at least not in head-to-head matchups with the talent and skill of black folk.

You've been handed a history where you got most of the land, made most of the money, got most of the presumptions of goodness, and innocence, and intelligence, and thrift, and genius—and just about everything that is edifying and white. So it's hard to stomach your gripes about the few concessions—surely not advantages—to black folk and other folk of color that are suggested in affirmative action. And the irony is that, in aggregate, when we add in white women and other abled folk, it is white folk who are the overwhelming beneficiaries of affirmative action.

That makes it sound like malarkey when so many of you complain that you aren't being treated fairly, either. You say that our demand for justice causes you unjust suffering. You think you miss out on jobs that go to less-qualified blacks. That may be one of the greatest claims to collective self-pity known to mankind, and yet you, with straight faces, keep telling black folk and others that we're the ones throwing self-pity parties around the country.

There is more, beloved. If black folk hurt because of race, you say you hurt because of class. Many of you can't see that race makes class hurt more. And when many of you claim that black folk shouldn't get affirmative action, that the kids of, say, Barack Obama, or some rich black person, shouldn't get a bid for a job or a space in a classroom usually reserved for white folk, you miss a crucial fact: wealthy blacks didn't get a pass from Jim Crow; well-to-do blacks don't get an exemption from racism. Of course our status mostly protects us from the worst that you can do to most of us, but it doesn't stop us as a class of folk from being denied opportunities that our smarts and our success should have guaranteed.

Another way you dilute black history is to make your-selves the heroes of our struggles. You argue that there have always been good white folk helping us out. Let's just call it dilution through distortion. It is the sting of noblesse oblige. Just look at the movies. Films about slavery must feature a sympathetic white character who wants black folk to be free. John Quincy Adams must be the real hero of *Amistad*, since Cinque couldn't rebel effectively without help from his great white defenders. *Ghosts of Mississippi*, about the mur-der of Medgar Evers, highlights the heroic white prosecutor, Bobby DeLaughter, who fought to open the case, and much less the brave black widow, Myrlie Evers, who fought white supremacy to make sure he paid attention. *Mississippi Burn-ing*, supposedly about the killing of three civil rights work-ers in the sixties, celebrates two white FBI agents, heroes in a state where white terror rarely had better allies than silent white law enforcement or brutal local police.

If such portrayals might be laid at the feet of last cen-tury's retrograde racial politics, the present is also flush with white savior movies. In *Free State of Jones*, Matthew McConaughey plays real-life figure Newton Knight, a poor farmer from Jones County, Mississippi, who galvanized a group of white army deserters and escaped enslaved folk against the Confederacy during the Civil War. And in *Free-dom Writers*, Hillary Swank plays a white teacher in Long Beach in the mid-nineties who educates nonwhite high school students in the midst of inner city hardship. With white friends like that black folk need no heroes of their own.

My friends, we cannot deny that white folk of con-science were of enormous help to the cause of black struggle.

Black and white folk often formed dynamic partnerships to combat racial inequality. But too often white folk want to be treated with kid gloves, or treated like adolescents who can't take the truth of grownup racial history. So we have to spoon-feed you that truth and put your white faces in our stories to make you see them, perhaps like them, or at least to consider them legitimate and worthy of your attention. Appealing to your ego to protect our backsides, that's the bargain many of us are forced to make.

Beloved, it's not just on the silver screen where you dilute and distort our history. In everyday life the refusal to engage black folk tells on you through your exaggerated sense of insult where none should exist. Many of you are "shocked, shocked!" that black folk have taken to reminding you that "Black Lives Matter." Some of you are just peeved, but others of you are enraged. That's because you're used to distorting and diluting our history without much frontal challenge. You fail to realize that the nation has already set the standard for determining which lives matter and which don't. Black lives were excluded from the start. The reason "Black Lives Matter" needs to be shouted is because American history ignored black history, didn't tell black stories. The founding documents of American society didn't include black life. When black folk say "Black Lives Matter," they are in search of simple recognition. That they are decent human beings, that they aren't likely to commit crimes, that they're reasonably smart. That they're no more evil than the next person, that they're willing to work hard to get ahead, that they love their kids and want them to do better than they did. That they are loving and kind and compassionate. And that they should be treated with the same respect that the average, nondescript, unexceptional white male routinely receives without fanfare or the expectation of gratitude in return.

✢ ✢ ✢

To argue that we matter is not to deny that there are things about us that have always mattered more than they should, especially how we look. Black folk now glory in what was once the source of our grief: our black skin. And yet the phenotypic differences among the races have made our culture stand out. With us, history was altered by color. Our skin, the economy of the epidermis, permits white America to dismiss us by differentiating us. But the world we made together, the history we forged in conflicted congress, bears forever the mark of our offending, yet transformative, blackness.

Our history, black history, has been denied, but it has never really been invisible. In fact we have always been the most visible thing about America. Everyone else, all of your kin, the white immigrants, assimilated. But by virtue of our very skin color, we stood out. Ironically, the very thing that bound us to slavery also made it impossible for us to hide, to assimilate, to pass gently out of an outmoded institution.

American history is the history of black subjugation. The Constitution is a racially hypocritical work of genius. The north and the south are divided because of us. The history of the twentieth century in America is the history of our struggle against white America. And yet nowhere, apart from South Africa under apartheid, is the omission of black folk from history as glaring an omission. Our presence is so saturating, so embedded, so inextricable, that white America's most reactionary, racist identities revolve around us—the Klan rally is grievous testimony to ineradicable black identity. And the most intimate and industrious spaces in white America, from the kitchen to the construction site, rest on our labor. There is no getting around blackness. In slavery, it was the intensity of our proximity—of white and black—that defined us. In that sense whiteness and blackness are an American invention. Our agency, our story, is linked to your history, your story. Black and white together.

Beloved, you must give up myths about yourself, about your history. That you are resolutely individual, and not part of a group. That you pulled yourselves up by your bootstraps. You must also forcefully, and finally, come face-to-face with the black America you have insisted on seeing through stereotype and fear. Whiteness can no longer afford to hog the world to itself or claim that its burdens are the burdens of the universe. You must repent of your whiteness, which means repenting of your catastrophic investment in false grievances and artificial claims of injury. You must reject the easy scapegoating of black folk for white failures, white disappointments, and white exploitation.

3.

THE PLAGUE OF WHITE INNOCENCE

Beloved, you are ensnared in one of the bitterest paradoxes of our day. You say we black folk are thin-skinned about race. You say a new generation of black activists focus too much on trendy terms like "micro-aggressions." You say they are too sensitive to "trigger warnings." You claim they are too insistent on safe spaces and guarding against hateful speech that hurts their feelings. You argue that all of us are too politically correct.

And yet you can barely tolerate any challenge to your thinking on race. I say thinking, my friends, though that is being kind. Many of you hardly think of race. You shield yourselves from what you don't want to understand. You reveal your brute strength in one contemptible display of power after the next, and yet you claim that we reap benefit by playing the victim.

To be blunt, you are emotionally immature about race. Some of you are rightly appalled at the flash of white racial demagoguery. Yet you have little curiosity about the complicated forces of race. You have no idea that your whiteness and your American identity have become fatally intertwined; they are virtually indistinguishable. Any criticism of the nation is heard as an attack on your identity.

But, my friends, your innocent whiteness is too costly to maintain. We are forced to be gentle with you, which is another way of saying we are forced to lie to you. We must let you down easy, you, the powerful partner in our fraught relationship. Your feelings get hurt when we tell you that you're white, and that your whiteness makes a difference in how you're treated. You get upset when we tell you that whiteness has often been damaging and toxic. You get angry when we tell you how badly whiteness has behaved throughout history.

But we must risk your wrath to speak back to a defiantly innocent whiteness. You often deem black dissent as disloyalty to America. But that black dissent may yet redeem a white innocence that threatens the nation's moral and patriotic health.

✢   ✢   ✢

"For the first time in my life, I feel guilty about being white," my student admitted in shame. His voice barely rose above a whisper. He hunched over in embarrassment, his cheeks flushing.

A momentary hush came over our sociology seminar. Our intimate setting gave us a stronger emotional connection than we might have had in a bigger class. The subject matter made our bond even more intense. We were studying how black folk died throughout American history. The readings opened my student's eyes to what he had never before been made to know.

I was torn. I wanted to honor his pain. I wanted the whiteness he had never confronted to fully wash over him, over me, over all of us in the class. I wanted the other white students to share his shame, if that's how they truly felt—or to find it a bit much, or to feel entirely unsettled by his confession of white guilt. I didn't want him to be alone in his head or feelings.

But I also wanted the students who were savvier about whiteness to speak up. Those who knew how whiteness often avoids direct hits; those who knew how whiteness often distorts the arguments of its opponents to make itself appear more reasonable, more natural; those who knew how whiteness escapes notice in a blizzard of qualifications meant to avoid responsibility. I wanted them in the stew with him to help sort things out. I wanted the students of color in the class to weigh in too. I wanted them to tell us if they were learning new things about black pain. Or to let off steam from a simmering rage at how white folk could afford not to know what many of them couldn't help but know.

I'd seen enough in life to know that remorse has its place in our moral ecology. But I didn't want my student to suffocate beneath an avalanche of guilt. White guilt changes nothing permanently, and bad feelings about black suffering don't last forever. They certainly can't remove the source of the shame. I wanted my student to know that whiteness is a problem to be struggled with, that it is a culture in which one comes to maturity, that it is an identity one inherits and perpetuates, that it is an ideology one might flourish under and, in turn, help mold, that it is an institution from which one benefits, an ethos in which one breathes, a way of life. For the rest of the semester we grappled with our guilt, our anger, and, for some of us, even our hopelessness, trying to make sense of it all.

My student's confession opened a way for us to say things that are often tough for white folk to say: that whiteness is a privilege, a declared, willful innocence, and that lots of white folk in our nation don't know the kinds of things we were learning in class. One of my bright black students got exasperated at how many white folk protected themselves from such knowledge by seeing themselves as the victims of hurt feelings.

"A lot of white people don't want to confront these issues, and as a result, we end up reinforcing white fragility," she said. It was the first time many in the class had heard the term. White fragility is the belief that even the slightest pressure is seen by white folk as battering, as intolerable, and can provoke anger, fear, and, yes, even guilt. White fragility, as conceived by antiracist activist and educational theorist Robin DiAngelo, at times leads white folk to argue, to retreat into silence, or simply to exit a stressful situation.

I have seen this in many lectures I've given over the years. When many white folk disagree, or feel uncomfortable, they get up and walk out of the room. Black folk and other people of color rarely exercise that option. We don't usually believe that doing so would solve anything. We don't trust that once we leave the room the right thing will be done. Plus we've fought so hard to get into most rooms that a little discomfort is hardly a reason to drive us from the premises. Such rooms likely affect our destinies, something that many white folk needn't worry about, because they have access to so many other rooms just like the ones they are leaving.

I have, over the years, developed a pedagogy of the problematic to address the thorny matter of race, whether it is wrestling with the burdens and sorrows that honest talk of whiteness brings or discouraging my black students from the easy retreat into sanctuaries of black solace. I want students to confront the brutal legacy of race with the kid gloves off, and yet respect each other's humanity.

Such an effort isn't easy. I get scores and scores of letters and e-mails from white folk who are angered by how my pedagogy of the problematic plays out in the media. They make sure to let me know what a moron I am, how unfortunate my students are to have me as a professor—okay, let's be honest, at times that might really be true—how Georgetown should fire me on the spot. They often call me "nigger" to remind me of the inferior status I keep forgetting to embrace. And many are mad because they say I am trying to warp young people's minds.

On that score they have a point. I seek to fix the warp that racial bigotry can bring; I want to challenge, one brain and body at a time, the poisonous precincts in which some of my white students were bred. I want my students to be uncomfortable with their racial ignorance, with their sworn, or unconscious, innocence. I'm sure that feels warped to many whites.

Teaching at a Catholic school like Georgetown has given me renewed appreciation for "culpable ignorance"—in this case, the idea that white people are responsible for things they claim not to know. Although I'm a man of books and thought, I'm also a man of faith. It is my faith that helps me see how whiteness has become a religion. The idolatry of whiteness and the cloak of innocence that shields it can only be quenched by love, but not merely, or even primarily, a private, personal notion of love, but a public expression of love that holds us all accountable. Justice is what love sounds like when it speaks in public.

✢   ✢   ✢

As my brave white student discovered, whiteness claims so loudly its innocence because it is guilty, or at least a lot of white folk feel that way. This is why, of course, your resistance to feelings of guilt is absurdly intense. There is a terror in accepting accountability, because it doesn't end with your recognition that something is rotten in Denver or Detroit. It suggests something is amiss across our country.

That's a terrifying thought to field, a terrifying responsibility to absorb. It means accepting accountability for your unanimous, collective capacity for terror, for enjoying a way of life that comes at the direct expense of other folk who are denied the privileges you take for granted.

If white guilt is real, so is black guilt, though it is quite different and has its own history. Black bodies that were captured and enslaved reached American shores half dead and soaked in racial guilt. They were guilty of their blackness, guilty of being dangerously different. They were guilty of resisting the loss of their freedom, guilty of their rage at injustice, guilty of trying to escape, guilty of the insubordination of indignation. They were guilty in every way of every crime, and whiteness, in adjudicating that guilt, told itself the very same lie every abusive parent, every batterer, and every spouse killer has told their victim throughout space and time: you made me do it.

And when this innocence is questioned, whiteness rages, or it weeps in disbelief. Conservatives lambast the moral and intellectual inferiority of blacks. Liberals cry at our ingratitude. How dare the historically guilty point a finger at the innocent? No court in the land can change the immutable fact of race, of guilt and innocence by pigment. It might be the *Dred Scott v. Sandford* decision that held that an enslaved man was his master's property and that blacks are not citizens. It might be the *Plessy v. Ferguson* decision that cleared the way for the separate but equal policies of Jim Crow. No matter the weight of white transgressions, they are seen as small acts of badness within a bigger body of goodness. "We have bad seeds," says the innocence narrative, "but those bad seeds only prove how good the plant is. A few of us are guilty, but only a few. The rest of us are innocent."

You preach responsibility as a personal credo, as a civic tenet, and yet you will have none of it. Your guilt is unbearable to you. But our daily subjugation, our not naming your guilt, is unbearable to us. We are unbearable to each other. And so we are stuck looking across a divide we cannot bridge.

What I ask my white students to do, and what I ask of you, my dear friends, is to try, the best you can, to surrender your innocence, to reject the willful denial of history and to live fully in our complicated present with all of the discomfort it brings.

Many of you find yourselves exhausted by thinking of how such colossal change might be made. You worry that your individual choice to do better won't be a match for our horrible history of hate. And even when individual black people confront individual white people, even when we love one another, white innocence still clouds our relationships. We are two historical forces meeting, and the velocity of that history is so strong that it can break the bonds of individual love. We are no longer two people asking each other to be understood. Instead, we are two symbols in a 400-year-old battle of guilt and innocence.

This happens to so many of us, so many of you. The white person we love is no longer an individual, but, in their insistence on innocence, they are all of whiteness; they have chosen whiteness over us. This may happen between loving black and white classmates in a college course that probes the history of race. In these encounters abstract ideas often become concrete realities. The beauty of history, its ornate, or ugly, truths, are distant until we are brought face-to-face with their consequences. History takes shape in the person before me. When it is made personal, history becomes urgent. The neat irresolution of history becomes messy, yearning for an answer now.

We are no longer ourselves alone. What was once the collective, institutional notion of whiteness becomes the white person I encounter. And my blackness is no longer isolated and atomistic; it forges destiny with all the blackness that came before me. And in my insistence on holding you accountable for privilege, for tiny but terrifying aggressions, for condescension, for any of the everyday racial slights that reinforce white supremacy, I have invoked again your sense of your guilt. I am not just a person, but a pointing finger, a scold, a challenge to the authority you were given as a birthright and that you cannot bear to relinquish.

If this can occur between classmates, between friends, between lovers, between blood kin, imagine the stakes when it occurs between groups of people. Whiteness becomes a mob of innocence and it responds like a mob to a call for black justice. It responds with riot gear, tear gas, clubs, arrests, Tasers, rubber bullets, and real bullets too. It responds with a collective *no*. In that moment of mob innocence, it truly believes that if one police officer is indicted, whiteness itself is indicted. If one mass shooter at a black church is brutalized or injured before he can reach a fair trial, then whiteness itself is injured.

White fragility is a will to innocence that serves to bury the violence it sits on top of. The fragility of ego versus the forced labor of slavery, the lynchings of Jim Crow, the beatings and the police violence sparked by the endeavors of desegregation. If it weren't real, if it weren't in action every single day—and every day seems to bring new stories of an unarmed black person being shot down by the police, new stories of black college kids being called "nigger," new stories of white anger flashing in bigoted humor about the first black president—it would be a perverse joke.

✢   ✢   ✢

Beloved, to be white is to know that you have at your own hand, or by extension, through institutionalized means, the power to take black life with impunity. It's the power of life and death that gives whiteness its force, its imperative. White life is worth more than black life.

This is why the cry "Black Lives Matter" angers you so greatly, why it is utterly offensive and effortlessly revolutionary. It takes aim at white innocence and insists on uncovering the lie of its neutrality, its naturalness, its normalcy, its normativity.

The most radical action a white person can take is to acknowledge this denied privilege, to say, "Yes, you're right. In our institutional structures, and in deep psychological structures, our underlying assumption is that our lives are worth more than yours." But that is a tough thing for most of you to do. My students are a bit of a captive audience. They're more willing to wrestle their whiteness to a standstill—or at least a tie between the historical pressure to forget and the present demand to remember. Believe it or not, that tiny concession, that small gesture, is progress.

Of course it is hard to undo an entire life of innocence and the privileges it brings. And so you play a game. You pretend that by accountability we mean that you are guilty in a very specific way of some heinous injury. For instance, when we speak of affirmative action, we are not saying that you are individually responsible for the bulwark of white privilege on which it rests. We are saying, however, that you ought to be honest about how you benefit from getting a good education and a great job because you're white. To twist that into the attempt to prosecute a case against all of white privilege through your individual story is an irresponsible ruse, and you know it, and yet you continue.

There is a big difference between the act of owning up to your part in perpetuating white privilege and the notion that you alone, or mostly, are responsible for the unjust system we fight. You make our request appear ridiculous by exaggerating its moral demand, by making it seem only, or even primarily, individual, when it is symbolic, collective. By overdramatizing the nature of your personal actions you sidestep complicity. By sidestepping complicity, you hold fast to innocence. By holding fast to innocence, you maintain power.

The real question that must be asked of white innocence is whether or not it will give up the power of life and death over black lives. Whether or not it will give up the power to kill in exchange for brotherhood and sisterhood. If it does, it can at long last claim its American siblings and we can become a true family.

✦   ✦   ✦

Beloved, fake regrets or insincere apologies for wrongdoing only reinforce white innocence.

I got a whiff of this sort of moral failure in 2015 when I watched the tribulations of Levi Pettit unfold in, of all places, Tulsa, Oklahoma. Tulsa has a long history of white oppression. In 1921 white residents of Tulsa massacred hundreds of black citizens and torched Greenwood, one of the wealthiest black communities in America, in a matter of a few hours in one of the worst acts of racial terror in the nation's history. Pettit, a University of Oklahoma student and former high school golf star, was caught on video chanting a frat song that exulted in saying "nigger." It also endorsed lynching. The gist of the ugly ditty he led on a bus trip to a party for his Sigma Alpha Epsilon fraternity was that a black person would never be admitted to the group. When the video went public Pettit was expelled from the university.

Pettit held a press conference at a black church in Oklahoma City to apologize for his racist behavior. The black leaders that he sought forgiveness from dutifully surrounded him. Pettit was performing a common three-step ritual of the remorseful: mess up, dress up, 'fess up.

The beginning of Pettit's mea culpa was promising. He thanked black state senator Anastasia Pittman, to whom he turned for guidance, for schooling him about the meaning behind his hurtful words. Pettit said he was sorry for his actions and admitted that there was no excuse for his behavior. He never saw himself as a bigot, but then, to be blunt, not many of you do. Pettit pledged to combat racism for the rest of his life.

The trouble started when Pettit was asked where, and from whom, he learned the nasty song. He waved the question off, insisting that he was there to address his actions and not the song's origins. That gesture was surely a sign of willful, durable white innocence. When he was pressed about what he was thinking as he mirthfully chanted the song, Pettit dismissed the question as immaterial to his apology. And yet he and his fellow fraternity boys were all enjoying themselves on the video. After only a few questions Pettit held up his hand, announced "I'm done," and quickly exited the room.

Pettit refused to address some of the most damning elements of his offense. Thus he took back with one hand what he had given with the other, that is, the willingness to confront racism head-on. Such a gesture is the prerogative of white innocence. My friends, there has been a great deal of talk, and no small consternation, about the idea of white privilege, the unspoken and often unacknowledged advantages that white Americans enjoy. And many of you are resentful of such talk; you think it is foolish. This was a glaring example. When Pettit stood at the lectern he appeared to take responsibility for his actions. In some ways he did, even as other culprits were hidden from view. That hateful chant was undoubtedly passed down through SAE generations as part of the fraternity's racist legacy, one that it clearly cherished. Pettit functioned that day as a scapegoat.

It is harder to indict forces and institutions than the individuals who put a face to the problem. Institutional racism is a system of ingrained social practices that perpetuate and preserve racial hierarchy. Institutional racism requires neither conscious effort nor individual intent. It is glimpsed in the denial of quality education to black and brown students because they live in poor neighborhoods where public schools depend on the tax base for revenue. Minority students, like the ones I teach at Georgetown, are more often beset by economic and social forces than overt efforts to deny them equal education.

Racial profiling is another strain of institutional racism. It is the belief that a person's racial identity, and not their behavior, is a legitimate reason to be suspected by the police of criminal activity. Redlining is yet another example. Until the late 1960s, banks marked certain neighborhoods on the map to show where they would withhold investment. Those banks also overcharged black and brown people for services and insurance, or encouraged them to take on faulty mortgages. The Fair Housing Act of 1968 outlawed redlining, and yet the practice persists, arguably leading to the largest loss of black wealth ever in the subprime mortgage scandal that triggered an economic recession in 2007. And even though the Voting Rights Act of 1965 guaranteed the franchise, the relentless assault on black voting rights through unprincipled and often illegal voter ID tactics complicate that right. These are institutional practices that extend racial hierarchies.

Beyond these institutional forces lie the symbolic meanings of public gestures. A pat on the back by one of the ministers gave the impression that Pettit was a victim in need of support and understanding. No such gesture was extended to the invisible sea of black students on campus, and across America, who had been antagonized by Pettit's racist antics or very similar behavior.

✢ ✢ ✢

My friends, sometimes the call of white innocence is far more insistent, far more explicit, far more unapologetic. And there are occasions where you have sought to hide behind a figure who gives bigger voice to your grievances and your fragility, to your angry insistence of innocence. In such instances you outsource it to a vile political figure who echoes your most detestable private thoughts. Even before the nation got a full blast of such a phenomenon, I saw it up close.

It was the summer of 2015, and there I was, in the lobby of the NBC building in New York, confronted with the flaming orange visage that is Donald Trump. I had just finished criticizing him on a daytime talk show when our paths crossed in front of the elevator bank.

"You've been *very* tough on me," the future president said. "But I love you."

There's no question that Donald Trump has "huge" charisma. He possesses a brutally appealing magnetism that, tragically, amplifies the most virulent rumblings of racism, misogyny, and xenophobia this country has reckoned with in quite some time. That is because Donald Trump is the literal face of white innocence without consciousness, white privilege without apology.

Each election, we hear that this run for the presidency says more about who we are than any other—Obama defines us, Reagan embodies us, Bush will be the ruin of us all. We've become inured to the get-out-the-vote sales pitch; the nation endures. And yet the 2016 election was indeed the most eventful of my lifetime, and perhaps the most important. Whiteness was at stake in a way it hadn't been in decades.

Trump's efficacy as an ambassador of unrepentant white innocence, and ignorance, and privilege, doesn't depend on whether his personal racial views add up to bigotry. What he's done in public will suffice to pass judgment. Trump's political popularity took off when he sullied the citizenship of Barack Obama, the nation's first black president. The "birther" claims were driven by unwarranted skepticism about the place of Obama's birth and the status of his birth certificate. Trump's recent assertion that Obama is an American still rang false and appeared as little more than an attempt to deflect responsibility for his vicious views onto his Democratic opponent, Hillary Clinton. His admission that he said Obama was born in America to keep his campaign going was a moment of ruthless honesty that sealed the case.

It is not simply a matter of voicing disapprobation for Trump; his supporters, too, must be answered. Many are driven by rage that for eight years a black man represented a nation that once held black folk in chains and that still depends on the law to check black social and political aspirations. Barack Obama so spooked the bigoted whites of this country that we are now faced with a racist explicitness that we haven't seen since the height of the civil rights movement.

Trump, more than anything else, signifies the undying force of the fear unleashed by Obama's presidency. He manipulates a confused and self-pitying white public. Yes, yes, some will say—but not all Republicans are like Trump. Not all of them even like Trump. It is true that parts of the Republican establishment finally, and unconvincingly, rebelled against Trump. But it was these same "reasonable" Republicans who ignored his early impact. They refused to listen to those who insisted that his vitriol was destructive to the country. As long as it didn't impact Republican, or white, interests, the lives Trump imperiled didn't matter. Now that he has been elected president, many Republicans have overcome their misgivings and enthusiastically returned to the fold. The party for which he is now standard-bearer must be held accountable for his creation.

It wasn't so long ago that Obama led millions of white Americans to believe that they were voting for a transformational figure. He would make the country permanently better. A vote for him was a vote for decency and intelligence, a vote against hate and chaos. It meant, simply, being on the right side of history.

Yet Obama's impact has been so quickly and thoroughly eclipsed by a pervading sense of racial and national doom. What many of us didn't see coming is that Obama's success would also be counted as his failure. The election of the nation's first black president tapped into a deep vein of escapist hope, that it would be a simple, painless way to heal our historic wounds. We projected onto Obama our desire to crush bigotry with enlightened democracy. Obama, a stalwart of social justice, a wonder of political rhetoric, would be the unifying force of national identity and speak redemption into our bones.

But too many of you, my friends, more than I could bear to imagine, resented Obama's rise. What we did not fully understand, or account for, is the deep-seated, intractable anger of the white Americans who never viewed Obama as either fully American or quite human. Donald Trump has exploited these people, promised them a different transformation, one that returns the country to what they would like to believe it once was: theirs. This is the naked, unapologetic face of white innocence on steroids. We have moved backward in so many ways since the high point of Obama's first election.

✥　✥　✥

The sort of willful innocence that Trump conjures is far more visible, and thus susceptible to opposition, than subtler visions of whiteness tied to American identity. For so many of you, what it means to be white is what it means to be American, and vice versa; your American identity is indissolubly linked to your whiteness. It is a possessive whiteness, too, one that hogs to itself the meanings of democracy.

Very little reveals the heart of innocent whiteness more than a challenge to professional football. It is a game that tests the durability, and rigidity, of American ideals of patriotism and national belonging. It is a game that also seeks, paradoxically, to cast out the very black bodies that have come to define the sport.

Beloved, this became clear with the uproar over the decision of San Francisco 49ers quarterback Colin Kaepernick to kneel, instead of stand, during the playing of the national anthem. He did so to protest injustice against black folk. Despite the backlash, Kaepernick says, "[I am] going to continue to stand with the people that are being oppressed. To me, this is something that has to change, and when there's significant change—and I feel like that flag represents what it's supposed to represent, and this country is representing people the way it's supposed to—I'll stand."

Kaepernick has been accused of being a traitor to the nation, a disruptive, self-aggrandizing narcissist, and a loathsome human being who disrespects the military. Clearly, it is still difficult to talk about race in an informed and intelligent fashion. And clearly conservative forces are arrayed against athletes, making it difficult for an athlete of color to forge ties to his people, and to speak out about issues that affect a significant portion of his fan base. My friends, can you not understand how this highlights the hypocrisy of a sport that has given second chances to players like Greg Hardy and Ray McDonald, who were accused of domestic violence? That warmly embraces Ben Roethlisberger, twice accused of sexual assault? And yet the sport is enraged at a player making a humane gesture of identification with the victims of racial violence?

Kaepernick has been criticized for his lack of patriotism. The accusation is nothing new. Black folk have been viewed suspiciously throughout American history because of a willingness to be critical of the nation even as they love and embrace it. How many of you who claim that Kaepernick is unpatriotic realize that many black men put on an American uniform and fought overseas, only to return home to be spurned and denied the rights for which they fought? How many of you realize that black soldiers who had fought valiantly for American liberties sometimes returned home to die on the lynching tree because racist whites resented them for wearing the uniform or hoisting the American flag? How many of you know that in 1976, the year of the Bicentennial, during a Boston City Hall demonstration against court-ordered busing, a white student protester turned an American flag, tied to a pole, into a weapon to viciously assault Ted Landsmark, a black lawyer?

✢ ✢ ✢

Black folk have, throughout history, displayed their patriotism by criticizing the nation for its shortcomings. And they, in turn, have been roundly criticized. The great abolitionist Frederick Douglass, who fled from slavery, offered a famous oration on the meaning of Independence Day, asking, "What to the American slave is your Fourth of July? I answer a day that reveals to him, more than all other days of the year, the gross injustice and cruelty to which he is the constant victim." The great black poet Langston Hughes grieved in verse, "There's never been equality for me, / Nor freedom in this 'homeland of the free.'" When Martin Luther King, Jr., said that America "is the greatest purveyor of violence in the world today," and opposed the Vietnam War, he was branded a traitor who, according to black journalist Carl Rowan, had created "the impression that the Negro is disloyal." Muhammad Ali was stripped of his title and run out of the ring for his conscientious objection to the Vietnam War.

Now all of these figures are celebrated: King's birthday is a national holiday and Ali was given a hero's burial not long ago. Michelle Obama, once pilloried as ungrateful and unpatriotic, is more popular than her husband, and Barack Obama, once assailed as unpatriotic for not wearing a lapel pin of the American flag, won not one but two terms.

My friends, none of these black figures hated the nation. Instead, they wanted the nation to straighten up and fly right. Douglass refused to join the chorus of black voices yearning to return to Africa and decided to stay put in

America. Hughes was hurt by America but longed for her acceptance when he titled his poem "Let America Be America Again." Martin Luther King, Jr., declared that white America had to do blacks right, yet he spoke for most of us when he said, "We ain't going nowhere."

What some of you are missing is that Kaepernick is the best kind of American there is: one willing to criticize his country precisely because he loves it so much. James Baldwin said it best when he wrote, "I love America more than any other country in the world, and, exactly for this reason, I insist on the right to criticize her perpetually." Both Baldwin and Kaepernick have offended you so greatly because they insisted on separating whiteness from American identity. The two are neither synonymous nor exhaustive; they neither signify all that America means, nor can they possibly radiate the full brightness of her promise. Donald Trump is missing the point when he says that Kaepernick should "find a country that works better for him." Instead, Kaepernick believes so deeply in this country that he is willing to offer correction rather than abandon the nation—and to donate a million dollars in support of racial justice causes. But innocent whiteness recoils at such instruction. It pushes back against the notion that it could possibly learn anything from a black body kneeling on white sacred territory. But it is that same territory that profanes and then swallows the bodies of unarmed black folk. We must see Kaepernick's criticism as love—the tough love that America needs. Even though his decision not to vote in the 2016 presidential election was a grave political miscalculation, Kaepernick's social protest remains a vital, valid gesture.

✛ ✛ ✛

The opposition to black displays of dissent rests on a faulty premise and a confusion of terms. Many of you who oppose our dissent because of patriotism are really opposing us because of nationalism, and, whether you know it or not, a white nationalism at that. There is a big difference between nationalism and patriotism.

Nationalism is the uncritical celebration of one's nation regardless of its moral or political virtue. It is summarized in the saying, "My country right or wrong." Lump it or leave it. Nationalism is a harmful belief that can lead a country down a dangerous spiral of arrogance, or off a precipice of political narcissism. Nationalism is the belief that no matter what one's country does—whether racist, homophobic, sexist, xenophobic, or the like—it must be supported and accepted entirely.

Patriotism is a bigger, more uplifting virtue. Patriotism is the belief in the best values of one's country, and the pursuit of the best means to realize those values. If the nation strays, then it must be corrected. The patriot is the person who, spotting the need for change, says so clearly and loudly, without hate or rancor. The nationalist is the person who spurns such correction and would rather take refuge in bigotry than fight it. It is the nationalists who wrap themselves in a flag and loudly proclaim themselves as patriots. That is dangerous, as glimpsed in Trump's amplification of racist and xenophobic sentiments. In the end, Trump is a nationalist, and Kaepernick is a patriot.

Beloved, there appears in this flap to be a confusion of symbol and substance. The worship of the flag is, too, a form of nationalist idolatry. It is not respectful love. It confuses the cloth with conviction. The power doesn't reside in the flag; it resides in the ideals to which the flag points. The worship of the flag gets us nowhere, nor does enthusiastically embracing the troubled song that accompanies it. Listen to the third verse of "The Star-Spangled Banner," which includes the words, "No refuge could save the hireling and slave / From the terror of flight or the gloom of the grave." Whiteness was pitched into the nation's collective memory through song in the same way that it was stitched into the nation's pride through a waving banner.

Most of us know nothing of our anthem's political pedigree or its racist implications. That's why American hero Jackie Robinson wrote in his autobiography, *I Never Had It Made*, "I cannot stand and sing the anthem. I cannot salute the flag. I know that I am a black man in a white world." What can lift the Stars and Stripes higher are the real-life practices that make that flag and that song meaningful. If we cite the Bible, and yet fail to live according to its codes, the Bible becomes just another book. But when we live it, it becomes powerful. If you believe it, the words of scripture say that we become living epistles in whose life others read the presence of God.

It should be clear to you, my friends, that American sports, despite all of the black bodies that make it go, is still a profoundly white enterprise. Surely you must see that it is only the court or the playing field that is integrated. Nearly

70 percent of football players are black; the NBA is 80 percent black. But the NFL's front offices in particular teem with white men whose outdated viewpoints and narrow understandings of race—and at times bigoted perspectives—hamper true progress. The players in football and basketball may be overwhelmingly black—and in the case of baseball, increasingly Latino—but the front offices of major American sports are a white man's game. For example, according to the Racial and Gender Equity Report Card for the Institute for Diversity and Ethics in Sport, in 2016 just 22.2 percent of professional administrator positions on National Football League teams were held by people of color. In the NFL's league office, only 9.4 percent of those with management positions were black in a league where nearly two-thirds of its players are black.

That may explain why, according to sports website *Deadspin,* anonymous NFL executives (it is interesting that they will not own up in name) say they don't want Kaepernick near their teams because he is a traitor and has no respect for our country, and "[expletive] that guy." Others state, "I have never seen a guy so hated by front office guys as Kaepernick." As long as black athletes keep their mouths shut and play the game, they're fine. Once they range beyond deference and obedience, they're out of bounds, and huge penalty flags are thrown.

Kaepernick's courage has also thrown a harsh light on some of the sport's biggest black stars—like Jerry Rice, Rodney Harrison, and Hines Ward—who have retired and now offer commentary. Harrison argued that Kaepernick's heart is in the right place, but that he's "going about it in the wrong way." He said that Kaepernick doesn't seem to realize that a lot of folk sacrificed to "give him the freedoms and the liberties he has," and that "sitting his butt down" during the anthem will only make folk mad. Harrison also attacked Kaepernick's racial authenticity, saying he wasn't really black, and claimed later he had no idea that Kaepernick is biracial. Was Harrison then suggesting that Kaepernick wasn't really black because he had no ghetto credibility?

The attempt to censor Kaepernick by citing his lack of racial bona fides is a tragic game that, once one begins to play it, can never be won, because there's always somebody blacker than thou.

Hines Ward also criticized Kaepernick for the manner of his protest. That instead of sitting down during the anthem he should give his entire check to the cause he believed in. Yet Kaepernick's method of disruption proves his point: giving a million dollars, or even his entire salary, may have showcased Kaepernick's generosity, but it wouldn't by itself have drawn attention to the underlying oppression that he is protesting. It would not have landed him on the cover of *Time* magazine as a patron saint of sorts for black justice. Legendary 49ers receiver Jerry Rice tweeted that "All lives matter"—a definite and well-known rebuke to "Black Lives Matter"—and that Kaepernick shouldn't "disrespect the flag." Rice later had a change of mind and tweeted his support for Kaepernick "bringing awareness for injustice!!!!"

Rice's evolution notwithstanding, these men do not realize how they have been seduced, how white innocence has made them accomplices in opposing blackness. They clearly don't understand that without some brave soul in the past like iconic running back Jim Brown speaking up at the "wrong" time, they wouldn't enjoy the perks of fame and wealth today. Without protest and social pressure the major sports leagues would not have been integrated. The criticism of Kaepernick by these former players reveals their astonishing amnesia.

Of course, the same astonishment and anger also greets those blacks who protest in the streets and are said to be disrespecting the police.

The two are yoked: criticizing police brutality is said to be hating law enforcement. Sitting during the national anthem is said to be hating America. This sophomoric approach will remain a roadblock to genuine racial engagement until it is replaced by a deeper, more humane, more sophisticated understanding of the issue of race.

The silence of white athletes must be challenged too. Prominent white athletes shouldn't leave Kaepernick out on a limb by himself. Those who are socially aware should speak up and challenge the narrow perspectives and white privilege that protects them. They must at least be asked to do so. The unawake and deeply apolitical black athletes, and the ones who mimic the conservative values of the white mainstream, must be called out too.

The best of our athletes have understood their responsibility to represent their people. They understood that their privileges meant nothing if others couldn't enjoy them as well. They knew that if their kin and community were disrespected, it was only a matter of time before they were too. They could not justify remaining silent by making great sums of money and being embraced by the dominant culture while the masses of black people suffered. We have seen black athletes turning away from black suffering because they believed they were merely individuals, and not also part of a group. That sort of black exceptionalism is illusory. One cannot ultimately be exempt from the treatment of one's brothers and sisters. They are you, and you are them.

The greatest mark of our humanity and character shows when we are concerned about others beyond our circle. The NFL dragged its feet in setting policy to address domestic violence long after it became a national issue. The NFL still has not received the message about racial violence and the injustice and oppression that prevail in our society. While the Rooney Rule, which mandates that teams interview minority candidates when coaching and senior football operations vacancies open, has not produced as many minority head coaches as wished for—teams still hire who they want—perhaps we can insist even more strongly that the rule be applied to the NFL front office. Teams should consider front office personnel with a balanced perspective on race, gender, and sexuality so that we might avoid the reactionary politics, resentment of difference, and the white panic that too often fills those spaces.

There's been a transition in sports from social activism to social service since the apex of social protests in the sixties. Today's athletes are discouraged from identifying with a progressive or unpopular cause, the way Bill Russell, Muhammad Ali, Jim Brown, Wilma Rudolph, Althea Gibson, Kareem Abdul Jabbar, and Oscar Robertson did in the 1960s when the civil rights movement was seen as destructive and disruptive. Their activism helped to break down barriers and increase pay and open doors for others, including those who hadn't protested. Still, we must not forget that they were strongly discouraged from their activism and harshly rebuked by the powers that be.

Since that heyday, leagues have begun promoting race-neutral charitable activities. Visiting a sick kid in a hospital is admirable, and a black athlete is often paired with a white child in an innocent, nonconfrontational setting. But that cannot replace speaking on behalf of black kids who are being gunned down in the streets by cops, or who are victims of the failures of the criminal justice system. Social service at times obscures the need for justice by confusing compassion with change. Martin Luther King, Jr., said that charity is a poor substitute for justice.

The white agents who represent black athletes have often undercut the value of social activism too. Many white agents counsel their players not to take on social issues. They are extremely careful about what causes may enhance or soil their clients' brands. While brand management is vital, their hesitancy to encourage principled protest by their clients means that commercial interests trump social conscience. A less charitable interpretation suggests that white agents who don't have deep investments in black communities are not motivated to address the plagues that black folk confront. These white agents fail to see the need of that athlete to speak up on behalf of the black and minority communities that nurtured and sustained them.

Kaepernick has bravely touched the third rail of American sport, one that we have not yet contended with. The status quo always favors neutrality, which, in truth, is never neutral at all, but supports those who stand against change. Cam Newton—the Carolina Panthers quarterback who refrained from saying whether he thought Kaepernick was right or wrong—may be superman on the field, but his response to Kaepernick's cause of social justice has kryptonite written all over it. We don't need Newton's signature dab gesture on the field; we need to fight for all folk to get dab off it. The real heroes, the real supermen, are those willing to take a stand, even if it means taking a knee while the national anthem plays.

✢　✢　✢

Beloved, your white innocence is a burden to you, a burden to the nation, a burden to our progress. It is time to let it go, to let it die in place of the black bodies that it wills into nonbeing. In its place should rise a curiosity, but even more, a genuine desire to know and understand just what it means to be black in America.

BEING BLACK

IN AMERICA

4.

NIGGER

Admit it, beloved, that word—that abomination—is still with us.

Yes, it's ugly. Yes, it's vile. Yes, it's full of hate.

And yet, a lot of you, or at least a lot of the folk you know, still think of black folk as *niggers*.

I remember the first time I heard the white world call me "nigger."

I say white world because it was not an individual man saying that to me, mind you, even though the words came from his mouth. This man was simply repeating what he had been told about me. I was every black person he'd ever meet. We were all the same. That's what *nigger* meant. That's what it still means.

It was 1965. I was seven years old. We and family friends were down south for a monthlong visit with our kinfolk. On that day I drove with our friends to see other relatives who lived hours away. In the backseat of the car my friend Johnny and I behaved like typical kids. We had quickly plowed through our brown paper bags of bologna sandwiches and our Mason jars of Kool-Aid. Soon our stomachs started to groan in hunger. A shiny diner appeared up ahead and we begged Johnny's parents to stop. Looking back I'm not quite sure what made them ignore their sense of the likely reaction we'd all face. I think the cumulative indignities of racism had finally got to them. It was absurd not to be able to eat the same food at the same time in the same place with white folk. I think they just momentarily snapped. Well at least his mother did. His father knew all too well the price he might pay for offending the white world with something as simple as his voice. His pleasing baritone was a threat to the tenor of the times. That's why he stayed behind in the car, while Johnny and I and his mother took a chance that just this one time some white person might be kind enough to treat us like human beings.

"We don't serve niggers here."

He didn't yell. His eyes were cold but his words were dry and matter-of-fact. He spoke them the way you might tell someone they'd reached a wrong number. But for me they altered the shape of my universe.

Even if we were "good niggers," we were still *niggers*. (That is why, when I preach, I can never say "good Samaritan," as though the distinction between a good and bad Samaritan, like the one between a good and bad *nigger*, rests on anything except what the larger world deems good, that is, subservient.) The strength of the adjective had no way of modifying the vulnerability of the noun. Blackness could never be good in a way that could help black folk because a *nigger* could never be of any service to himself if he were busy living down to expectations. It was a wash from the start. If you accepted the term *nigger,* no speech or grammar could rescue you.

Johnny's mama, a beautiful, high yellow woman, grabbed our hands and yanked us back out the door faster than we could walk.

"What's a nigger?" Johnny asked. "What's a nigger?"

I had never heard the word either. I lived in a world where blackness poured over us like warm molasses and filled our ears with affection, where black love didn't have to be spoken to be felt. But I knew when the spell was broken and we were hurled into a parallel universe of quiet hate.

"What's a nigger?" Johnny asked a third time.

In that instant I knew exactly what it meant. It was a tidal wave of foul water crashing down on me, staining me, choking me, and pulling me out to the point of no return. I knew it was a condemnation, not just of me and Johnny and his mama, but of every black person I loved, the ones I didn't like, the ones I didn't know, the ones I would never know. In that moment my mouth filled with the taste of hate beyond anything my parents or any adult in my life could fix.

Surely you won't judge me, beloved. And please don't make a silly false equivalence between us. Some of you claim that black folk are racists too when they use epithets like honky, redneck, cracker, ofay, gray boy, and the like. But you know that's a lie, and I'll tell you why a little later.

Don't be taken aback by the wash of hatred over my pre-adolescent mind. Can you blame me? I was a seven-year-old child feeling the weight of the white world's hate crushing my precious soul. There was no Benjamin Spock to explain the trauma I endured as a grade school victim of hate. There was no Jean Piaget to explain the impact of utter revulsion on my cognitive development. I would quickly learn how others of my race fended off your grave assault. A famous black leader told me how he and his young adult peers would rifle through the obituary section in the white papers and gleefully proclaim "another cracker gone." I heard churchgoing folk who love the Lord sanctify their rage with holy profanity at your barbarous mistreatment or murder of us. "Goddamned crackas. Motherfucking honkeyass ofays. Fuck all of them redneck peckerwoods."

"What's a nigger, Mommy?" Johnny asked for the last time in utter exasperation.

His mama knelt down between us, her eyes level with ours, still holding our hands.

"Don't tell your Daddy," she said to Johnny. She turned to me.

"Promise you won't tell, Michael. And promise you won't tell your Daddy when we get back. Both of you, promise." We promised. We stood there and swore the oath of secrecy that too many mothers and children of my era were compelled to swear. I knew from her worried eyes, her tight lips, her urgent tone, and her painful grip on my hand that this moment, this word, in this context, could never pass from my mouth to my father's ears, even as it echoed in mine. When my father died in 1981 at the age of 66, I had not broken my promise.

Nigger.

I don't remember what lie Johnny's mother told her husband about why we didn't bring back any food. I do remember that she didn't want me to tell my father what happened because that knowledge—the knowledge that his son, his family, was in danger—was a black man's kryptonite. Men like Johnny's father and mine were still young enough and full enough of dreams inspired by the north's meager but real freedoms that the treatment of black people in the south could lead them to act, as southerners would say, foolishly. The danger was always there. Even small gestures like being dismissed, or disrespected, or scorned made a black man taste his bitter limits. Forced to be less than they were, to be less than men, to witness the white man's silly insistence that they eat from a different lunch counter. It all might suddenly be too much to bear. A man might snap at the awareness that he couldn't protect his family, not really, not like white men. For a black man, the knowledge that his son and his loved ones had just been called *nigger* could turn, swiftly, to calamity.

I entered a dark room of knowing when Johnny's mama swore me to silence. I began to realize that a word alone could sap my father of his powers. It could rip the cape off his manhood and he could no longer be his family's superman like all good daddies deserved to be. It was not because he couldn't leap tall buildings in a single bound. That was easy. I'd seen him jump the tall homemade doghouse in our backyard in pursuit of a huge rat that threatened to bite us as we played. It was not because he was not more powerful than a locomotive. My father's nickname was "Muscles."

It was because there was one thing that Superman did that my father couldn't do, and while I didn't know it, I sensed it even then, when I still believed in Santa Claus and the Tooth Fairy: my father wasn't faster than a speeding bullet, or more powerful than a noose. In that moment I inherited black intuition, a sense about the world that outpaced my knowledge of it. It was black intuition that, in retrospect, was inevitable because all black people get it at one time or another. It is passed down from generation to generation in the cellular memory of our vulnerable black bodies. I got my innocence snatched from me, with one word, more abruptly and years earlier than white children lose theirs. And for all that my own story is specific, it is the opposite of unique.

✢   ✢   ✢

Nigger.

That one word. I know you recoil at its use. I know you have never used the word yourself, or at least almost never. You may admit, however, that, unfortunately, some of your kin have used it, especially the unlettered ones, or the previous ignorant generation. You know the ones. It's mortifying, isn't it? I know you hate its use in polite white company. You may even have called out a friend who used it. You think *nigger* is a linguistic fossil. It belongs in the museum next to the Confederate flag.

You watch the documentaries and docudramas about O.J. Simpson and his infamous murder trial. You nod your head in agreement with the plea of black prosecutor Chris

Darden that the court not air a recording of racist white cop
Mark Fuhrman uttering *nigger* because it is the "filthiest,
dirtiest, nastiest word in the English language" and it will
"upset the black jurors." (Of course you overlook, or ignore,
how, as Darden speaks, the camera zooms in on Simpson's
handsome face, his furrowed brow and impish smirk suggesting a "nigga please" response to Darden's declaration.)

You are proud of your principled stand against the use
of hateful language. If the word must be referenced, it needs
to be verbally castrated, stripped of its hostile spelling and
snipped into harmless abbreviation. *Nigger* limps into the
"N word." My Lord, how you contort language; my God,
how we demand that you do. You bend over backward gram-
matically to avoid the appearance that you for one moment
tolerate bigotry. Yet the bigotry the word refers to remains
in place. It is understandable that many of you cannot say
that word, at least not in public, and never in front of black
folk. We have made it clear, well, at least most of us, that we
find it unacceptable for white folk to say it under any condi-
tions. But despite all your effort and care, the word is still out
there, still wreaking havoc, even when it's not being spoken.

Nigger condenses the history of hate and the culture of
violence against black folk. When white folk say the word
they bridge the gap between themselves and the hateful history it reflects. It links verbal and physical violence. The term
is also a form of moral violence. It has to do with the inten-
tions of white folk when they hurl that word in our presence.

Beloved, I am not arguing there is evil magic in white
lips to call down violence with words. The word *nigger* has
such fantastically evil resonance because there is a kind of

moral onomatopoeia at work: *nigger* is a word that comes as close as any to suggesting the racial violence that it describes. *Nigger* says lynching, castration, rape, rioting, intellectual inferiority, Jim Crow, second-class citizenship, bad schools, poor neighborhoods, police brutality, racial terror, mass incarceration, and more.

Nigger has no rival. There is no rough or refined equivalence between the term and the many derisive references to white folk. Those terms don't evoke singularly gruesome actions. *Nigger* is unique because the menace it implies is portable; it shows up wherever a white tongue is willing to suggest intimidation and destruction. There are no examples of black folk killing white people en masse; terrorizing them with racial violence; shouting "cracker" as they lynch them from trees and then selling postcards to document their colossal crimes. Black folk have not enjoyed the protection of the state to carry out such misdeeds.

The state, in fact, rendered black folk even more vulnerable. White racism was the government's science project; bigotry was its nightly homework. Evil flashed a white face in a terrorizing *crackerocracy,* an exuberantly diabolic band of proud haters of black culture composed of the Klan, the White Citizens Council, neo-Confederate outfits, white nationalist groups, and the legions of unaffiliated fellow travelers. Their mottoes differ, but *nigger* is the rallying cry for all of them. We must effectively respond in our day to the ugly persistence of racism, even if its form has changed.

So what are you supposed to do?

My friends, what I need you to do—just for starters—is not act. Not yet. Not first. First I need you to see. I need you to see the pains and possibilities of black life, its virtues and vices, its strengths and weaknesses, its yeses and nos. I need you to see how the cantankerous varieties of black identity have been distorted by seeing black folk collectively as the *nigger*. It is not a question of simply not saying *nigger;* you have to stop believing, no matter what, that black folk are *niggers* and all the term represents. Instead you must swim in the vast ocean of blackness and then realize you have been buoyed all along on its sustaining views of democracy. What would this nation be without the efforts of Frederick Douglass and Martin Luther King, Jr., to make it behave according to its ideals? What would it be had not Diane Nash and Fannie Lou Hamer given their all to quench the fires of hate?

You must not only deal with familiar black persons, but with blackness per se, with blackness as a moral arc, with blackness as history and culture, with simple yet profound black humanity. You may discover after all that we, black and white, are far more alike than you suspected—or feared. Your fear that we are just alike may cause you at first to doubt, but then, defensively, to embrace the lie of black inferiority your people have practiced from the start of our experiment in democracy.

I sometimes think of how the *nigger* crawled from the newly forming white imagination as a denial of everything that was enlightened and human. I also think about how Frankenstein is the name of the scientist and not the monster, but the monster soon came to be identified by his inventor's name. "Whiteness," in the same way, may be the true *nigger*. Stitching together a warped reflection of yourself, each piece a rejected part of your own body, the creation is made *from* you, not just *by* you—a despised version of all your imperfections. Like the monster Frankenstein, the *nigger* is kept animate as much by the white fear of becoming, or, in a manner, of always having been, the thing it hates most, as by a competing fear: that it should lose control of a part of itself, yes, a black part, and a despised part, too. The loss of control is glimpsed in the black desire to be anything except the *nigger* that whiteness has made black folk out to be.

Yet many of you, beloved—honestly, it may be most of you—pretend not to know any of this. It may be that you don't know many of us. You've got one, two, perhaps three really good black friends. Maybe you're not pretending. Maybe you don't know because you don't want to know. Maybe it's worse. You don't have to know. Your life hasn't depended, like ours has, on knowing what the "other" likes or dislikes.

Black folk have had to know white culture inside out. We know what coffee you like, what mood you're in, whether you'll be nasty or nice to us on the subway. We know just by how you glance at us as you interview us if we'll get that job. We know the fear you feel when we get on the elevator, so we whistle Vivaldi or the *Andy Griffith* theme song to put you at ease. Although, just to spook you, we sometimes ask the black person we're with how he's adjusting to life after being locked up for murder for the last 20 years.

We know the way you clinch your white girlfriend a bit tighter when our virility marches up on you unannounced, and the woman on your arm, you fear, will want to be in our arms. So we act less threatening. We have to know as much as we can know about you to keep you from wrecking our lives because you had a bad day. We have to know all we can know about you to keep you from firing us or gentrifying our communities and shipping us to the outer perimeters of hell. As the creator of a bad racial allegory, you have all of Dante's rage but none of his poetry.

✢ ✢ ✢

Beloved, we know the word finds greater currency and menace in white circles than you are willing to say. The ban on its use by white people is an attempt to arrest its murderous spread. The white folk who claim that the call to stop using the word is to cave in to political correctness ignore history and black humanity. They are the kind of whites who pose as "honest."

We have, most of us, anyway, rejected your imagining and defaming of us as *nigger*. We have done everything humanly possible to prove that we are not who you say we are. I am from a generation far more willing to make the effort than the one freshly on the scene. Black Millennials have little use for respectability politics; they see no need to prove their humanity before you treat them with decency. They discern the fatal lapse in your logic: Why should black folk ever have to prove our humanity to white folk who enslaved and raped us, castrated and murdered us for kicks?

Your white humanity is forever at stake with such young folk. And you know what, beloved? They have a point. Black folk my age and older have a direct memory of what it means for white folk to be blind and deaf to us even when we stood by the thousands in the streets and screamed our names for the world to hear. "I Am a Man," we blared through a bullhorn, amplifying both our desperate desire to be recognized and our unknowing sexism. While pleading that the world not be blind to us, we couldn't see the women by our side. "I Am Somebody," we insisted, even when it was more aspiration than belief. All of that was our way of saying—in reality, our way of preparing to proclaim—that "Black Lives Matter."

Beloved, there is something black folk fear, whether you can see it or not, whether some of us black folk will say it or not. Our fear is that you believe, that you insist—finally, tragically, without hesitation, with violent repercussions in tow—that, in all sorts of ways, we are still your *nigger*.

It is a belief you hold on to all these centuries later. It is a belief that has survived all of the marches, and bullhorns, and protests, and politeness, and good behavior, and forgiveness, and Kumbaya, and nice Negro smiles. It has survived our dancing to a song playing nowhere except in our heads. It is a song that we hoped would quiet your insistence that we disappear or die. It is a belief that has survived all our trying, trying, trying to make you see that most of us will never do you any harm. And you've shown a brutal consistency through the centuries by not hesitating to kill a *nigger* on sight.

It's painful when black folk have so easily, sometimes unknowingly, perhaps invisibly, bought into the logic of the *nigger* and let it rule our minds. I saw this in my own family.

When I got into Cranbrook—a prestigious prep school outside of Detroit in Bloomfield Hills, one of the wealthiest suburbs in America—my parents and I took a tour of the school's prosperous geography. As a white student guided us around campus, we weathered a light drizzle and came upon a puddle. The white kid stepped around it, and I stepped right through it since it wasn't deep.

"See Ivory, the white boy is a genius, and Michael ain't," my father said to my mother, thinking I hadn't heard him, or, perhaps, he didn't care whether I heard or not.

A great grief engulfed me. It was at that instant that I completely, unforgettably, understood what Baldwin meant when he wrote of his own father that "he was defeated long before he died because, at the bottom of his heart, he really believed what white people said about him." I felt the same about my father. He was a barely literate man who likely had to drop out of school in Georgia in the eighth grade. He was a man whose industry and muscles got him work in a factory. He was proud of my desire to get more education, yet he lived in a prison of disbelief in his own worth. Therefore he doubted mine too. That he could believe that a white kid was smarter than me because he stepped over a puddle proved how little he believed in black intelligence and how much he bought the lie of white superiority.

I flashed back to when I was eight years old and I mimicked his pronunciation of the number four. He pronounced it "foe." I followed suit, but he stopped me in my tracks.

"Don't you go to school, boy?" he asked me.

"Yes," I replied.

"Don't you know how to say that right?"

"Yes."

"Then do that from now on. That's why you go to school."

I could feel his self-doubt mingled with his deep desire for his son to do better than he had. But at Cranbrook that day his self-doubt led him to take refuge in caustic judgment. He projected his limitations onto me even as he wanted me to have more opportunity. This is the racial catch-22 that too many of us face. This is what whiteness does to the black mind.

✢ ✢ ✢

I saw what being thought of as a *nigger* did to my father. I also see what it does to millions of my people who struggle every day to be recognized as human beings.

But I'm different, right? You may think you know me. That I'm a middle-aged man with a PhD, a minister, a public intellectual, a media personality. That I am an exception to your idea of blackness.

I am burdened and privileged by this idea of me, your idea of me. It is a fiction that traffics in long-held beliefs about race. My privilege rests on the idea that I am special, that I am different, that I'm not like "them." That difference is partly why I get to address you directly, beloved. Why I am considered more capable of speaking to the problem of race, more articulate than "regular" black folks.

But I am not this fiction. I am like every other black American, a person caught between two perceptions. A Jekyll and Hyde of race. Dr. Jekyll is the professor that many of my people, and many of you, love. Mr. Hyde is the black man who grew up on the streets of Detroit, who needs do little more than return home to see a fate that could have become my fate in the face of my brother Everett, locked behind bars for more than a quarter century now.

Everett and I are the two black Americas. I am black America the way white America tells us it *could* see blackness *if only*—if only we were all respectable, successful, prominent, institutionally affiliated. My brother is the way America *does* see blackness—suspect merely for existing, naturally violent, obviously criminal, rightly sentenced, thankfully incarcerated. He is my brother and we are two sides of a family coin, a coin that is both biological and national. I don't for a moment buy the false dichotomy between us. We are both tied together in a seam of racial destiny as the *nigger*.

I am reminded of this almost daily as I get letters and e-mails from hateful white folk. Choice examples include: "You and that worthless POS in the White House have brought back and given new meaning to the word nigger!" "You Dick head Dyson, you really are a Fucking Nigger." Or I'm a "spear-chucking, blue-gum, steppin-and-fetchin', uncle Tom, field nigger. Get your ass out there and pick some cotton while your mammie cooks some chitlins. Your books are shit just like you." (I don't doubt that even some legitimate critics feel that way.)

An especially sensitive writer weighed in with the belief that "[w]hites will always beat niggers down because they are black savages." Another fan opined: "You being an educated man, I have always felt that you were the worst kind of

Nigger, (asshole) smooth talking bastard though you may be." Another writer could barely stand to pen anything in the body of the e-mail; the subject line said it all: "Shut the fuck up nigger." Yet another said, "You define the word nigger." One pen pal said, "[You are] nothing more than a hate filled nigger that was given your position due to the politically correct morons that believe you can give self-respect to those that have no idea how to earn it." Another told me that hip-hop "is just niggers talking shit to a scratched up record." (Okay, I have to admit, that description does fit a few rappers.)

Beloved, this is just the tip of the iceberg of hate. This is why I can never pretend that I'm in any way better than the masses of black folk. I know that no matter how much education I've got, how well I behave, how much compassion I show to white folk, how well-heeled I am in polite company, no matter how articulate I am, I am still just a *nigger* to so many white folk. And it's not just the lunatic fringe that swells with bigots. I'm afraid that angry white folk who consider themselves part of the white mainstream have just as much venom and ire. When I used to appear on Fox News pretty regularly with Bill O'Reilly, I begged him to say on air to his sizable audience that even though he disagreed with me, they shouldn't send me hate mail and call me "nigger." He never made that plea. His silence reinforced the racial social contract forged by angry whiteness.

And yet we have the ability to shatter that social contract. You must stop believing that you can't understand us, when, in fact, you choose not to understand us. You must stop seeing us as monolithic and therefore fundamentally, irrevocably different from you when we are singular and exceptional in all ways. Just like you. Our troubles will only cease when you stop believing what you know is untrue: that we are always poor despite our home-buying drive that makes you flee to the suburbs. When you stop believing that we are radical when we can be more conservative than you, that we are one color when we are a plethora of shades, and that we are related to each other and not you when you are related to us in more ways than you can count or may care to know. We are, finally, not your *nigger*, not in the best world we can create together.

Like it or not, black humanity has been, and continues to be, the only salvation white American humanity has. Democracy might well be a wounded bird incapable of flight without the poultice of black forgiveness pressed to its wings. When we confront racial catastrophe, black folk insist on fighting back. We have given this country the spiritual will and the moral maturity it lost in the bitter divorce of principle and practice. Our nation can only reach its best destiny when that recognition grounds our shared culture and existence. We want what you want. We want to pursue our dreams without the hindrance of racism. We want to raise our children in safety and send them to good schools. We want our communities to overflow with opportunity and support. We want good jobs and health care. We want gorgeous parks and lovely homes. We want affordable markets and department stores nearby. And we don't want to die at the hands of either the cops or other black folk.

5.

OUR OWN WORST ENEMY?

Beloved, why is it that every time black folk talk about how poorly the cops treat us you say that we should focus instead on how we slaughter each other in the streets every day? Isn't that like asking the person who tells you that they're suffering from cancer to focus instead on their diabetes? Your racial bedside manner has always been fairly atrocious.

But we are not fooled. You do not bring this up because you're genuinely concerned. You want to win points in debates. You want to avoid any responsibility for how traumatized our communities are. You want to hide from the horror of cops mowing us down like we're animals.

So you hurl that accusation at us like religion. But there is no righteousness in your retort, no healing in your hubris. We are dying, it is a serious matter, and you must lay down your smug self-satisfaction that we are our own worst enemies and face how you are killing us.

Just this once set aside your litany of accusations and listen. Just this once take the side of the true victims of oppression. Just this once please don't side with the manufacturers and perpetrators of our death. I'll be honest and admit that there are ways that black folk are doing ourselves in. But I hope you can admit that even those ways are often linked to our gutless embrace of the bigotries you spew.

✢   ✢   ✢

Do you think we like being killed by folk who look like us? Do you think it doesn't bother us? Our bullets are often aimed at each other because we're too near the site of pain and heartbreak, frustration and depression. We often lack food and shelter, and we live in homes overrun with bodies, leaving us little room or rest. So we lash out at them, or at an acquaintance, or a partner in crime. Yes, it is true: sometimes we send them, or, perhaps, a stranger nearby, to their eternal reward. This is the geography of despair. It is also the pain of never having control, of always being afraid, of struggling to care for and love what we cannot protect. I learned this lesson in a perilous way.

"Give me your money," the tall, slender black man demanded of my fiancée and me. We were near the corner of a Detroit ghetto street not far from where the '67 riots were sparked a decade earlier. It was cruelly ironic that we were close to the entrance to a Detroit police mini-station. We were walking home at 10:30 p.m. one Saturday night after a late choir rehearsal at church. Our assailant had come out of nowhere. He announced himself ominously with a .357 Magnum revolver at the end of his shaking hand.

Terror washed over us. This was the Detroit of the 1970s, the city that had been dubbed "the murder capital of the world." It was also a city in transition. America's manufacturing strength had showed the first inkling of bowing to a thriving service economy. All those well-paying factory jobs that had been an elevator to the black middle class would slowly begin to disappear. Coleman Young became the city's first black mayor in 1974. He won in large measure by promising to reform a brutal police force. Most white folk scampered to the suburbs after the riots in '67. That left black folk in charge of shrinking resources and facing the rise of drug gangs and a spiking crime rate. I feared that night becoming one of its casualties.

"Sir, we don't have any money," I said. "I literally have a dollar thirty-five cents to my name."

The man had on a pair of dark sunglasses. I couldn't see his eyes to gauge his demeanor. All I knew is that I didn't want my fiancée and I to die that night. She was scared speechless. I feared that any sudden move might cause him to shoot and kill us.

The Spirit urged me to talk to him. We'd just come from church. Why not call on faith to see us through?

"Man, you don't look like the type of brother that would be doin' something like this," I offered, praying it struck a chord of humanity, and, at least, racial intimacy.

Thank God it did.

"I wouldn't be doin' this, man," he said, his voice trembling, his body language suggesting a growing regret about his action. "But I got a wife and three kids, and we ain't got nothin' to eat."

It would be another year before my son was born into poverty and I'd know the desperation a father faces when he can't provide for his own child. Both his mother and I would be unemployed by the time he arrived. I'd have to stand in the WIC line to collect free food offerings. But for now I was focused on getting to that future.

Then our would-be robber delivered a real shock. He revealed the vicious cycle of carnage that makes some people victims and then pushes them to make others its victims, as well.

"Besides, last week, somebody did the same thing to me that I'm doin' to you."

"I tell you what," I said. "We just came from choir rehearsal. And if you'll let me reach into my back pocket, I can give you my church bulletin. It has a number you can call to get some help."

He took the bulletin and briefly glanced at it. He looked stumped, perhaps half in disbelief at my desperation, perhaps half believing that I really wanted to help him. I made my final offer.

"Look, I only have a dollar thirty-five cents, but I want to give it to you."

"No, man, you need that yourself."

"I insist. Take it, please."

He told us we could go free and to walk to the end of the block. I froze. I didn't want him to shoot us in the back. I asked him to get on his knees. I don't quite know why I asked, or why he complied. But, miraculously, he did. I said a very brief prayer for him. I didn't want to test the Lord's mercy or the man's patience. He stayed on his knees as we walked away, unharmed.

Beloved, I know what you're thinking. You're not considering how social deprivation leads desperate people to act desperately. You're not thinking of how communities bereft of hope and resource claim as its victims the people who seek to escape its fatal grip. You're not thinking of how many of you were spared such a fate because of God's grace and white privilege. Many of you are thinking that black folk kill each other every day without saying a mumbling word. Then we loudly protest a few white cops who kill black "thugs."

Former New York mayor Rudy Giuliani tried to ambush me with that "it's-the-blacks-not-the-cops" claim on *Meet the Press*. It was right before the decision was made not to bring charges against white cop Darren Wilson, who had killed unarmed black youth Michael Brown in Ferguson, Missouri. "I find it very disappointing that you're not discussing the fact that 93 percent of blacks in America are killed by other blacks," Giuliani said. "We're talking about the exception here."

The notion that we are indifferent to murders by other blacks is nonsense. But we also know that if Jamal or Willie kills somebody, and they're caught, they're going to jail. Cops are rarely held accountable for their slaughter of black people. Neither Jamal nor Willie pledged to protect and serve the community. Neither of them has been issued a badge and a gun to represent the state. The police have a higher standard to meet, a greater obligation to be cautious in using lethal force.

Black folk do protest, to each other, to a world that largely refuses to listen, the killing of blacks by other blacks.

We cry out against what goes on in black communities across this nation. We think it is horrid. We know such communities are vexed by problems faced by all neighborhoods that are depleted of dollars and hope. These communities are emptied of good schools. They are deprived of the social and economic buffers that keep Beverly Hills from turning into Beirut. People usually murder where they nest. They aim their rage at easy targets.

Beloved, what you see happening among us is not best understood as black-on-black crime. Rather it is neighbor-to-neighbor carnage. If our neighbors were white, they'd be victims of the same crime that plagues black folk. You are right, however, about those proportions. Ninety-three percent of black folk who are killed are killed by other black folk. But 84 percent of white folk who are killed are killed by other white folk. It's not necessary to modify the noun *murder* with the adjective *black*. It happens in the white world too. Where's the white-on-white crime rhetoric? Where are the rants against white folk ruining white culture with their murderous ways?

One truth should be clear: If you want interracial killing you have to have interracial communities. Wasn't that one of Martin Luther King, Jr.'s dreams? To live in a nation where black and white folk could be victims of crime in integrated neighborhoods? Didn't he argue that thieves should pay more attention to the content of our Cadillacs than their color? Perhaps I am misremembering?

White folk commit the bulk of the crimes in our nation. And, beloved, it might surprise you that white folk commit the most violent crimes too. According to FBI statistics, black folk committed 36 percent of violent crime in 2015, while white folk committed 42 percent of violent crimes in the same year. White folk consistently lead all other groups in aggravated assault, larceny, illegal weapons possession, arson, and vandalism. And white folk are far more likely to target the vulnerable too. White folk lead the way in forcible rape. You're also more likely to kill children, the elderly, significant others, family members, and even yourselves. White folk commit a majority of gang-related murders too. A majority of the homicide victims in this country are white. White folk are six times as likely to be murdered by a white person as they are to be taken out by a black "thug." The white-on-white mayhem is profound, yet no one speaks of it in racial terms.

That's because the phrase white-on-white crime doesn't serve a larger ideological purpose. White-on-white crime does not jibe with the exclusive focus on a black-on-black narrative that conservatives, and liberals too, have bought into. The success of that narrative depends on a few things. You had to construct the ghetto as a space of savagery that was unique to black folk. Never mind the fact that its first occupants were the Irish, Poles, Italians—and especially the Jews. Then you had to say that any right thinking folk wouldn't kill each other.

But there is no inherent blackness to the crime that occurs in black communities. Take blackness out of the equation and you'd have social engineers and Ivy League professors trying to fix crime-infested communities. We know this because big brains and social reformers from the late 1800s well into the 1930s successfully addressed crime waves set in motion, and endured, by poor European immigrants. Keep blackness in place and you have social engineers and Ivy League professors blasting the intrinsic pathology and inherent depravity of black life. These experts will conclude that our families and neighborhoods produce the seeds of their own destruction. The 1965 Moynihan Report on the Negro family—a report by Harvard professor and Johnson administration official Daniel Patrick Moynihan that warned that a castrating black matriarchy and a "tangle of pathology" threatened the black family—is a famous example.

Beloved, you don't stop there. You feel compelled to make crime merely a matter of ethical collapse. You don't mention the systemic removal of goods and services that drive some folk to crime. Nor do you talk much of black folk lacking the social supports that other ethnic groups enjoy. There is hardly any mention of the failure of the markets that are supposedly neutral, but which, in fact, favor those who aren't black or poor.

Beloved, let's try a brief thought experiment. Let's apply the logic of some of your arguments about black folk to you. Take your argument that we should pay more attention to black-on-black crime than white cops killing black folk because more blacks are killed by other blacks. Now let's compare the number of white Americans killed by whites to the number of Americans killed by terrorist acts. I can already feel your hair standing on end. You see how hurtful it is to make such a comparison? You see how it could miss the point of giving each cause of suffering its due? According to your logic, we should not be concerned with political acts of terror committed on American soil because, since 9/11, less than 100 people have been killed in such attacks in America while 11,208 people were killed by firearms in 2013 alone and 21,175 died by suicide with a firearm.

By Giuliani's logic, then, the obsession with terror is both misplaced and hypocritical. We should focus instead on the plague of firearms on the American population. Far more white folk kill each other than are killed by terrorists. So let's stop worrying about terrorism and worry about white-on-white homicide. Stop griping about a couple of planes crashing into a couple of towers. Stop crying over a few folk getting butchered by a few religious fanatics when the routine crime that snuffs white life lies in a white man's assault rifle.

Notice how just reading those words makes your blood boil? See how your nationalist bravado flashes? Can you imagine how your rage might spill over if that were said to you with the same callous disregard for white life that Giuliani speaks with when he dismisses cops killing unarmed black folk? See how your temperature rises by just reading those words? These are words that are rarely spoken directly to white America. Words that reflect back to you your dishonesty and indifference and tone-deafness to our plight.

✣ ✣ ✣

Beloved, I must admit that there are ways that black folk do aim hate at each other, ways we do rip each other apart. A lot of it has to do with how we've taken into our minds and souls the poisonous bigotry you've spread. It's brutal and agonizing to watch, especially because we are imitating the hate for blackness, for "otherness," that you taught us. But you seem hardly aware of this sort of black-on-black crime. Could it be that you don't really care about black-on-black crime unless you can use its existence to attack us even more?

But there is some value to you in our folly. You can point to it and say, "See, black folk are just as bad as us. They're even more destructive and hateful to each other than whites have ever been. See, just as the song in the Broadway play *Avenue Q* says, 'We're all a little bit racist.'" (Of course that's a horrible misuse of the term. Better to say we're all just a little bigoted, yes, or prejudiced for certain. But I'm afraid you've got to own racism all by yourselves, beloved. It signals the power not only to hate, but to make that hate into law, and into convention, habit, and a moral duty. Thank God brave Americans challenged the legal and ethical roots of racism in this country.)

You even find comfort in exploiting black prejudices—against darker black folk, against women, against queer folk, against poor folk. You feel good about it because it lets you off the hook as well. It's as if you take glee in thinking black people are equally bigoted. Especially when you hear one of us tell our dark-skin children not to marry a dark-skin mate so they won't have dark children. Or when you hear one of us say that only light-skin people have "good hair," or that there was no homosexuality in Africa and that it's a white man's plague.

We have sometimes been faithful proxies of white supremacy. If you'd take the time to know us, you'd see that we've imported some of the harmful beliefs you've laid on our psyches. Or we've generated our own varieties of troubling blackness. In fact, your racist dogma was so appealing that even when you stopped barking it, we demanded more in our own cultural quarters.

The ventriloquist effect of whiteness has worked brilliantly; black mouths moving, white ideas flowing. What your vast incuriosity about black life keeps you from knowing, and this is heartbreaking to admit, is that we black folk often see ourselves the same way you see us. Sometimes we view our own culture, our traits and habits, through the distorted lens of white condescension or hatred. Often we make other vulnerable black folk in our midst the *nigger* you've made us all out to be.

This came home to me after I battled bias at Carson-Newman. The racial dynamics of the college were troubling. Black students couldn't have been more than 6 percent of the student body. We weren't warmly welcomed either, except if we played ball. When I asked why there weren't more black speakers at the mandatory Tuesday chapel, it came down to crude mathematics: our small percentages mandated only one black speaker a year. Most of the other black students accepted that as par for the course; I was a few years older so it rankled me a bit more. I didn't enlist their help. I formed a one-man quiet protest and refused to attend chapel. In return for my resistance—chapel was mandatory—I was unceremoniously booted from the school after my junior year.

Then I had to figure out what to do to support my family. I had worked all through college, cleaning and degreasing heavy machinery at a local factory. Later I pastored a couple of different churches. After getting my walking papers from Carson-Newman, I got "called" to a bigger black church in East Tennessee.

I went there thinking that I had found my life's purpose. After being expelled from college, I was eager to apply my knowledge of the Bible and my beliefs about social justice in the black church setting. The only thing I really discovered is that God has a mighty sense of humor. The church I took charge of is named Thankful Baptist Church. They proved anything but grateful for me.

I decided that I'd challenge the black church's sexism. It was another show of our moral hypocrisy, another way of looking down the ladder at the face and fate of the *nigger* beneath us. The sad irony of our sexism is that it targets the women who make up the vast majority of our congregations. Of course I wasn't foolish. I knew that I'd have to teach for at least a year to get the church ready to ordain three women as deacons for the first time in its history.

In weekly Bible study, I hammered away at the parallels between sexism and racism. If God respected all people the same, then we had no right to deny women equal standing in our sanctuaries. All seemed well until a group of local ministers got wind of what I was doing and deemed it destructive to black Christianity.

"You gonna let this yellow nigga come down here and destroy the black church?" their leader asked members of my congregation.

"Y'all got to do something." So they did.

When I got to the church one Sunday morning, my key didn't work. *Must be fixing the door finally*, I thought. The key to my office didn't work either. *Finally*, I thought, *they are getting around to refurbishing my sparse quarters.*

I preached my sermon and couldn't help but notice faces I hadn't seen before. I thought my preaching was winning new converts. Apparently God wasn't one of them.

After church, a deacon rose to announce trouble.

"Pastor, there's a real problem in this church."

"Deacon, let's deal with that trouble."

"The problem is you."

Oh damn, I'm the trouble. Well praise the Lord and pass the offering plate because this wasn't looking too pretty for me.

The church erupted in applause, and then, in short order, took a vote to cast me out. It really hurt that most of the women in the church sided with their men against me and their own best interests. But I eventually understood; they had to live with those men long after I left.

✢　✢　✢

I thought I had heard the Lord clearly when I got kicked out of school. I thought I'd become a church pastor and preach the prophetic word of God. I thought I'd lead the people into the vineyards of progressive theology and together we'd be a mighty witness for the black church, challenging all of the ills of society. I thought first we'd uproot the ills in our own ranks.

But mine was the only uprooting. I was sent packing with a month's severance pay. Once again I was left with no means to support a wife and a preschooler.

I had little choice but to return to Carson-Newman and the bastion of whiteness from which I had been expelled to complete my education. I knew my return meant that I had to attend chapel regularly, but after my experience at Thankful Baptist, it seemed a harmless requirement. I had obviously heard God wrong.

It wasn't just gender that proved to be a barrier, a real source of suffering for black folk, not only in my church but across the nation. The shade of skin was a problem too. The minister who led the charge against me was, like me, a yellow Negro, and by citing my color in his theological brief against me, he shined a light on the deep wound of colorism in black America. The "light, bright and damn near white" black person is often put into conflict with the darker and richer chocolate members of our community. I had seen up close how color-struck black folk are.

My father was a hulking man known for his brawn and his blue-black skin. As I grew into adolescence and my understanding of the white gaze deepened, I saw how you looked at him. I couldn't help but notice how so many folk saw my father not as a man, but as a specimen, a hominid whose dark skin and outsized muscles conjured all the ruinous images of black folk fresh out of the jungle. Savages. Savages who woke at dawn to go to work to fuel the engines of your civilization. Savages without whom you could not turn the gears of the very world you demanded black bodies make for you.

After he was laid off from the factory, my father worked as a janitor and all-around utility man at a local pharmacy. I saw how the white owner of the store eyed him. The man valued my father's epic strength. But at the same time he infantilized my father. I even heard him once say to my father that he acted like a boy. I half expected my father to lay him in his tracks and prayed he wouldn't do so. Yet I was angry that he hadn't done so to preserve his sense of dignity and manhood. This same black man who was so tough on us kids didn't say a word. It gave me a hint of the psychic costs of black manhood, of thrusting and parrying with the cold facts of white dominance that hushed one's rage and yet encouraged it to flow against one's own family. I suspect that my father's suppressed rage found an outlet when he encouraged his sons to box each other, with gloves on but no headgear, to the point where we bloodied each other's noses in our ghetto basement. This was a poor black man's therapy.

At age seven, on our family trip south, I imagined what the word *nigger* might make my father do. At age fifteen, I saw in the pharmacy what it did to him. The word didn't just exist in the air, to be brushed away like a gnat because he knew better. It resided in him. It resided in all of us. We black folk also viewed his dark skin with cruel disregard. He was the *nigger*, not just to you, but to us, too, because we have learned to see through your eyes. I saw what seeing himself through your eyes did to him. It ate at him. It circled his mind and frisked him like an abusive cop. I saw that he had chosen my golden-skinned mother—he called her "Ivory"—at least in part as an escape from the prison of his own darkness. In black life light skin is valued because it is closer to your white skin, and those with it are deemed to be closer to your so-called civilizing influence. That very notion reeks of barbarism, reeks of a crude, primeval equivalence between epidermis and humanity, reeks, therefore, of white supremacy.

Sometimes my father beat us something awful. It was ritual and tradition, of course, in so many of our communities. He got beat, and, therefore, he beat. It had long since passed into rite and folklore, long since been an artifact of the agonizing anthropology of complicated black domestic habits. It had now become part of the art of punishment and control—in part to keep us from being slaughtered in the white world. The logic is as simple as it is brutal: I will beat my kids so white folk won't kill them.

That's some black-on-black harm you never seem to take credit for. That's some abuse rising from fear you never seem to take notice of, even a little responsibility for. You ever consider this, beloved? You ever have to apply the cane, or stick, or switch, or belt to your kid's backside for that reason? You certainly took the high road when it came to football player Adrian Peterson brutally switching his son. But you have no idea of the history of corporal punishment among black folk and some of the reasons it exists. Do you see how this might enrage us against you even more? We are angry that fear leads us to hurt our kids. We are angry that even after beating our kids, sometimes with sadistic regard for your criminally intense need to monitor us, you still manage to find ways to kill the flesh of disciplined black people.

White folk created the world where black whipping was necessary. White folk also created the world where black parental punishment is seen as savage. Our disciplinary practices are used to argue our questionable moral and mental health. Some of that may even be true. But white folk hardly ever want to admit they have a hand in all of this; you never assume responsibility for making it so. When my father beat me, I wondered if he was really flailing at himself, at an idealized self that was reflected in my lighter body but always beyond his reach. *Nigger* didn't just happen to us. It happened in us. Your continued acting on it and our internalization of it destroys us both.

As it did my younger brother.

Named after our father, Everett, a nutmeg brown, was a couple of shades lighter than him, but among the darkest of us boys. He adored our father. He loved whatever Daddy loved and wanted to do whatever Daddy did. My father loved cars, and when Everett was young, he built and raced go-carts. Competitive and bright by nature, he not only built the best go-carts, but brought them to victory more often than not. Once he was old enough, he traded go-carts for real cars and you could see him side by side with my father under a raised hood on a hot summer day, hands covered in motor oil, a rag hanging from the pocket of his faded blue denim overalls.

When Daddy died in 1981, none of us was ready. It deeply affected all of us. But Everett was the one who was broken by it. With our father gone, he seemed to lose his grounding. Like me, he had always been thoughtful and reflective, but where I read books, he read the streets. We both saw the corruption and injustice of the system we lived in, but while I sought to overcome it, he sought to beat it at its own corrupt game. He sold drugs. He thought he could outsmart the system. But in 1989, at the age of 27, he was tried and convicted—I believe wrongly—for murder, and sentenced to 25 years to life in prison. He has lived behind prison walls ever since.

I cannot blame his imprisonment on skin color, but I can say that how he was treated before he got locked up put him in a prison of sorts too. Like our father, his dark skin marked him for special treatment of the kind no one wants. When we were young, like so many dark-skinned boys, he was often predesignated as the troublemaker. He didn't finish high school, and got his diploma a few years later in prison. The bad *nigger*. It was assumed that he'd be more violent, more likely to do wrong, most likely to "catch a case" and commit an act of crime. If enough people, white and black, treat you like the *nigger* for long enough, you can start to see yourself that way. His life, like our father's, was lived in reaction to that word.

I saw, too, the favor, sometimes subtle, sometimes glaring, that my yellow skin got me. I saw how the teachers warmed up to me while spurning darker children. I saw how foreboding racial mythologies haunted the classroom, stalked the social settings where black folk lived. The teachers didn't give some of the darker kids the nod like they gave me; the darker kids didn't get the benefit of the doubt of being smart. I saw how it ruined many a Negro. I saw how many dark-skinned kids weren't encouraged in the larger society to believe that they had the skills they assumed I possessed just by glowing in the skin I had.

I also felt the resentment projected onto my light skin, a resentment of light privilege. It cuts both ways, for sure, but too many yellow Negroes deny light privilege the way many of you deny white privilege. We are as blind to our perks as you are to yours. Since I had a very dark father, I was forced to confront the ugly disputes over color that are often silently waged in our communities. But too many light folk just don't admit what we all know to be the case. And I'm not speaking of light guilt, our color-struck version of white guilt. I mean owning up to the benefits and advantages of being light-skinned. We make up the same reasons why we should be spared reckoning with shade and tone as you give for not addressing whiteness and privilege.

Our being color-struck isn't the only sign that we've imitated whiteness. We've also emulated and adopted your coarse reactions to class and sexual identity. Many of us have joined the unfortunate assault on gay folk. We see them as moral poison, or, more politely, we fault them for failing to cast aside a sinful lifestyle. Many black folk use the Bible to thunder down judgment on gay or lesbian folk. We trot out some of the same arguments that were used against black folk by white preachers: that God frowns on their sexual identity; that the Bible says their habits and desires lead right to hell; that their moral corruption is a blight on the community. We black folk have often said, just as you have, that we love the sinner but hate the sin. That questionable formulation proves to be even more ridiculous when applied to queer folk, whose sexual identity singles them out for judgment. For those of us who oppose gay marriage, our hypocrisy screams even more loudly. Although we deny it, the same kind of people who opposed interracial marriage oppose same-sex marriage too. And they are often armed with the same sorts of arguments. Black folk have blindly followed a path of prejudice that earlier ended with us as victims. Many of us find the abandonment of queer black folk a special breed of hypocrisy; failing, for the most part, to find a suitable social scapegoat for our distress, we realize there is no bottom rung that is not already occupied by another black person, and, therefore, we make new *niggers* of them. If, as Toni Morrison says, it is on the backs of blacks that America has been built, then surely blacks have built other forms of blackness, acceptable blackness, by offering *nigger* status to those we deem beneath us. As surely as fringe black figures like right-wing ideologue Rev. Jesse Peterson see the black poor as *niggers*, some religious blacks see queer folk the same way. We can't seem to shake our hypocrisy, and thus end up mimicking the whiteness we claim to despise.

✢   ✢   ✢

The use of nigger *has been* eerily consistent in the culture, especially with the presidency of Barack Obama stoking resurgent white panic and the emergence of Donald Trump amplifying white paranoia and racial belligerence. But black folk haven't stood by passively. A great many of us have tried to rob the word of its essential viciousness by reappropriating it, though, to many black folk, the effort smacks of internalized racist self-hate. They feel the effort is futile, and tips our caps too eagerly to a word that should be banished from the culture. A *nigger* is a *nigger*, or a *nigga*, they say.

Beloved, many of you don't understand why black folk ambushed the word *nigger* and made something strangely beautiful of it. What's more, you often appear upset that we appropriate this term while denying you the pleasure of helping us to reshape its use. We strictly forbid you the privilege of participating in our fierce disputes about the word. As for the attempt to make the word palatable in our arenas, you don't have to know a lot of social theory to know that powerless people often fight power with their words.

Black people have been lying in wait to murder *nigger* from the start. (Except for those who seek to become the *nigger* you feared in their rebellious or wayward existence, but that is something to explore another time.) We quietly fumed at the way the word caricatures our humanity. For a long time we couldn't make you stop using it so we gave it a go ourselves. Jay Z explains in one of his songs the mechanics of how the word went from *nigger* to *nigga*. Jay warned on the song "Ignorant Shit" that artists often use exaggeration to make their meaning clear. He boasts we "shoot niggas straight through the E.R." That is, he lopped off the "er" at the end of *nigger* and replaced it with the "ga" to make it *nigga*. Thus an offensive word became to many black folk an affectionate one.

Nigger is the white man's invention; the gender is deliberate here, since this was a white male creation even as white women shared the culture of derision too. *Nigga* is the black man's response since black men were most easily seen as *nigger*. But black women bore an even greater burden with a double portion of slander when they were called "nigger bitch." *Nigger* taps into how darkness is linked to hate. *Nigga* reflects self-love and a chosen identity. *Nigga* does far more than challenge the white imagination. *Nigga* also captures class and spatial tensions in black America. *Nigga* is grounded in the ghetto; it frowns on bourgeois ideals and spits in the face of respectability politics. That's why an incident in the last year of Barack Obama's presidency resonated so widely.

"Yo, Barry. You did it, my nigga."

Larry Wilmore fired a rhetorical shot across the bow of blackness with these words at the 2016 White House Correspondents' Dinner. The *Nightly Show* comic made an appearance before the group to tell jokes following President Obama's final standup routine. Referring to the president by his youthful nickname was one thing. Referring to him with a vernacular offshoot of *nigger* was something altogether different. Letting that be his last word about Obama at a gathering the world paid attention to was beyond the pale.

The fallout in black America was swift and heated. Black social media was atwitter with Wilmore's comments, supporting or lambasting him with equal passion. Black journalists and civil rights leaders chastised Wilmore for breaking black code and saying *nigga* in mixed company. They believed that Wilmore should have observed the informal rule that you don't say that word around white folk. But that rule was from before rap albums gave the term currency far beyond the hood. Wilmore's black critics reprimanded him for his poor choice of words and for insulting the most powerful man in the world. They also blasted him for disrespecting the black journalists in attendance. Others saw the debacle from both sides. Obama was unfazed by Wilmore's utterance. The smile on the president's face said that he enjoyed this spontaneous moment of racial intimacy. Obama returned Wilmore's "peace out" double fist pump to the chest and embraced him after his performance.

On the surface, the Wilmore controversy appeared to be little more than a skirmish between black elites over the use of politically incorrect language. In truth we got a glimpse of something far older, far bigger, and far more intense: the fierce battle to define black identity—indeed blackness itself—that has raged in black quarters since black folk set foot in the New World. The word *nigga* captures that tension.

Nigga often sounds organic and sensual in the mouths of black folk. Its meaning is shaped by the circumstance in which it's said. It is a term that works best when spiced with humor and slang. It is a greeting. "What up nigga?" It is a direct object noun. "You my nigga if you don't get no bigga." It is meant to emphasize or celebrate. The set up: "Hey man, I just got into Harvard." The celebration: "Nigga!" It is an imperative suggested by a change in tone. "Hey, bro, my doctor just called and said I've got to get some blood work." The speaker is urged to comply with the doctor's wish in a responding voice that slightly stretches the first syllable: "Nigga!" It is laughter. "These girls never give me any play and I drive a Mercedes, as in Mercy 'deez payments killin' me!" The humorous response, with hand over mouth: "Nigga!" It is a sign of approval: "My nigga!" It is a sign of disapproval, said sternly with squinting eyes: "Nigga." It is an expression of disbelief spiked with a smirk: "Nigga, please!" It expresses self-hate, much like *nigger* does, with a scalding, scolding tone: "Niggas." And it signifies a love for one's folk even as one acknowledges their flaws, largely in a light-hearted vein: "These niggas."

If more of you understood that *nigger* is a world apart from *nigga,* and if you understood how the different spelling and pronunciation—and the race of the user—changes its meaning, then some of you might not insist that you should be able to say it too.

Beloved, feel free to admit it. Most of you thought that black folk were saying *nigger.* You thought that you had been banned from using it because it was a horrible word, only to discover, to your surprise, that black folk were saying it too, which meant that it was once again safe to say. But many of you felt disappointed. You felt it your duty to admonish black people that they should know better since the word supports the bigotry of some whites. Too many whites believe that it is easier to warn black folk not to use the word *nigga*—to tone down their lyrics and eliminate a troubling word—than it is to keep white folk from using a racist epithet that still echoes in white quarters. Some of you may even feel a bit of anger since you had done so much to keep your family and friends from using the word. You think it is hard to tell white folk not to use the word when black folk simply won't stop.

My friends, white privilege screams in many of these reactions. The fact that too many white folk don't know the difference between *nigger* and *nigga* is more than a lack of curiosity; it is a refusal to learn about black life and culture.

Of course, it cannot be denied that some black folk also think there's no difference between *nigger* and *nigga*. But even though that's true, the stakes are different. Many whites draw equivalence between the terms as a way to establish fair rules about what blacks and whites should be able to say to each other. Many of you believe that the ban is universal and means nobody should use the word. Many blacks agree. Their aim is largely pragmatic. They want to keep white folk from believing they have a right to say the word in public. If the best way to do that is to keep black folk from saying it too, then so be it. That history sets some black folk's teeth on edge. They think the term's mutation to *nigga* offers scant relief from the hateful charm of *nigger*. They think that many of you won't be smart enough to tell the difference between the two. This may be where black conflict merges with white privilege. I refuse, and I hope you do too, to turn white Americans into infants. Older members of your communities know, or can easily learn, that there's a difference in the two terms.

Is it reasonable to say that younger whites who hear the relentless thump of *nigga* on their favorite rap tunes are ignorant of the history of violence against black folk that *nigger* suggests? Is it possible that those same black artists are poor historians too? That may be true. Yet those same kids, indeed those same artists, can't be let off the hook for refusing, as my father used to say, to "get their lesson." We don't excuse young people their ignorance of American history; we teach them, even as we chide their bluster and their pride in not knowing.

I had to testify in the 1990s before a state legislature about the effects of rap music on our nation's youth. I had to answer in part the claim that a white boy had been encouraged to use the "N word" because he heard it in his favorite music. I asked the legislators, rhetorically, if that same boy, who had been introduced, perhaps, to the "B word" too—which is repeated, arguably, as much as the "N word" in rap music—had refrained from using the term against, or around, his mother. I supposed out loud that he had no doubt learned how and when and with whom to use the epithet, or even one of its offshoots like "beyotch" or "biotch." Thus he learned not to use the B word in certain contexts, and should understand that he cannot use the N word either. The same is true for other white boys. Even as they hear the word *nigga* constantly looped they should know better than to abscond with the privileges of blackness tucked into their oversize clothing. I'm sure you realize the hypocrisy of urging folk to be responsible and yet making excuses for white America.

You may have heard some black folk argue that using *nigga* is a sign of black self-hate. That is black folk denying their own history, denying their own savvy, their ability to code-switch and to make distinctions between words and the histories those words carry. There are many signs of black self-hate to combat, but using *nigga* isn't one of them. Martin Luther King, Jr., the greatest black man ever, and arguably the greatest American too, used *nigger*. The night before he was murdered, King had a pillow fight with his lieutenant Andrew Young and his closest friend Ralph Abernathy. King and his compatriots often let off steam with such antics as they confronted the heart of American darkness. During the pillow fight, King playfully reprimanded Young, asking, "Lil nigger, where you been?" It is not that King is beyond the possibility of self-hate; a compelling argument for that resides in his little-known yet tragic disdain for dark-skinned black women. But self-hate certainly could not be ascribed to King for humorously using *nigger* as he was about to sacrifice his life for black freedom.

✣   ✣   ✣

Beloved, you've got to face the fact that accusing black folk of perpetuating the legacy of inequality by using *nigga* is a vicious ruse. It is yet another way of refusing to accept responsibility, of wanting everyone else but white folk to practice the accountability you preach. All of this is a calculation to avoid a bigger issue, and that is how black folk are, after all of our efforts to be accepted as fully American, still seen as the other.

6.

COPTOPIA

Beloved, some of you seem genuinely surprised that most black folk fear the police. You are sometimes shocked that we think of them as a brutalizing force. You cringe when we say they are out to do everything but serve and protect us. You think we are manufacturing stories about our bad encounters with police. You think that we must have done something wrong to provoke such remorseless cruelty. And yet we have exhausted ourselves telling you how they mistreat us so routinely that it is accepted as the way things are and will always be.

We learn how to modify our speech in the face of cops. We temper our passion and modulate our tone so that we barely register as being there. Do you have "the talk" with your kids to warn them within an inch of their lives not to sass the police for fear that they will return home to you in a body bag? I don't mean the usual conversation all parents have with their kids about respecting the cops. Sheer terror and outright fear motivate our discussions.

If you're old enough, and your birth certificate says "Negro" like mine does—from the early 1900s to the early

1980s all African American birth certificates labeled us as such—you'll know it's the same way we were taught to speak to white folk in the south. You keep that kind of manual in your backpack? It tells you to make sure to lower your eyes, say yes sir, no smart mouthing, no anger, no resentment, just complete, total compliance without a whiff of personality or humanity. Ever had to endure that humiliation, my friends? We must believe that cops are gods; we are nothing. And the more we remember our nothingness, become experts in the philosophy of nothingness, the better chance we have to survive. Does any of this sound familiar to you? It is our routine, our daily ritual of survival.

When I was seventeen years old, I was with my brother Anthony and a childhood friend, both a year older than me, and we were stopped by four Detroit cops. They were patrolling the neighborhood in an unmarked police vehicle. This was in the mid-seventies when we cowered in the shadow of the infamous Detroit Police Department task force called STRESS (Stop the Robberies, Enjoy Safe Streets), which was instituted after the 1967 riots. The unit certainly brought a great deal of stress to black folk in the streets of Detroit. During its two and a half-year existence, STRESS was accused of killing 22 citizens and arresting hundreds more for no good cause. White cops routinely targeted poor black communities. Ours was no different.

The big four amplified their command for us to get out of the car over their blaring megaphone. Then they approached us. The plainclothes officer snatched me out of the backseat. We were no strangers to their menace and naturally assumed the position against our car. The plainclothes officer who had yanked me from the car announced that our Ford Galaxie appeared to be stolen. That much was true. It had been stolen and returned to us more than a month prior. But the police had retrieved the car without removing it from their list of heisted vehicles. I wanted to quickly, but carefully, prove that the car had been legally returned. I wanted to prove that it belonged to our father, and that we had the proper ownership documents for it. I was quite nervous. Two of the officers had drawn their guns. We had all been frisked.

"Sir, I am reaching into my back pocket to get my wallet that has the car's registration," I said to one of the plainclothes officers. Before I could fetch it the cop brought the butt of his gun sharply across my back and knocked me to the ground.

"Nigger, if you move again without me telling you to I'll put a bullet through your fucking head."

I rose to my feet. Slowly. Deliberately. Showing complete deference. Barely breathing. Barely raising my head above a supplicating bow. Having mastered my body, having, basically, whipped me, lashed me on the plantation, the officer granted me permission to retrieve what felt like my freedom papers—the car's registration. But that registration was proxy for my breath. The cop permitted me to live. That was the victory.

The cops ran the tags, and less than fifteen minutes later, they concluded what we already knew: the car belonged to my father and we had the right to drive it. They offered no apology, and without a single word, with just a nod, they sent us on our way.

This was hardly the first time I'd had encounters with the cops, all bad, all with the promise of punishment for the slightest gesture of manhood, all with the possibility of violence lurking in the air.

Could you take that, beloved? Could you believe that most cops are good and well-intentioned when the history of harm forever hangs above your heads?

My friends, many of you have no idea of this level of anguish. You think that if we merely obey the cop's commands he or she won't feel threatened by us, won't view us as the roadblock to their return home that night. You think that if we keep ourselves in check nothing bad will happen.

Where have you been? Have you not seen the videos? These videos make it possible to see what has always been the case. Now there is proof of our suffering. Have you not seen how no matter what we do the cops come for us? That no matter how pleasant our speech, how lowly our spirits, how tame our bodies, how domesticated our gestures, we are read as a menace and threat by so many cops? "I feared for my life," many cops who have shot unarmed black folk have said. Not a gun in sight. No attack in the offing. And yet we are consistently, without conscience, cut down in the streets.

Can you honestly say that if we just comply with the cops' wishes that we'll be safe? How many more black folk do you have to see get sent to their deaths by cops while doing exactly what they were told before you'll believe us? You've seen the video of the young black man in South Carolina who goes to retrieve his wallet just as the Highway Patrol trooper instructs, and yet is still filled with lead for no other reason than he is who he is—a black male, a ferocious subversion of all that is decent and humane and worthy of space on earth.

How can we conclude anything different? How can you? If you're honest you'll see that the police force is a metaphysical collective with a gift for racial punishment that has never viewed black folk as human beings, because the law that they are charged to enforce has never seen us as human beings. And the Constitution that the law rests on did not write us in as fully human.

Can you truly say that you can't understand why most black folk fear, sometimes hate, the police? I've experienced that humiliation on a number of occasions. They've embarrassed me in front of my brother and my son. Most painfully, they've embarrassed me in front of myself. Every encounter with the police splits us into two selves, one a quiet, brooding figure cursing the cops from within, the other a dawdling doppelganger, a concrete-staring, shuffling Negro we are ashamed to admit lives inside of us.

Terror and shame go hand in hand. There is fear in realizing that we are helpless to persuade others that we are human. In that moment, there is also deep shame, shame that you do not take our humanity for granted. We are ashamed that there is nothing we can do to keep you from seeing us as worthless.

✦   ✦   ✦

I felt that same shame when I was a graduate student at Princeton in the mid-eighties. I was excited that my eight-year-old son Mike had come to visit me during the Christmas holiday. I hadn't had the chance to see him a great deal since my divorce from his mother in the early eighties. I wanted to do father things with him. Catch up on movies. Play a few video games. Toss a football or play catch with a baseball and mitt. Do some reading together.

On the first day of his visit, Mike and I headed over to my bank to get a cash advance on my MasterCard. I handed the young service rep my card. I felt good since I'd just paid my bill a couple of weeks before. He disappeared into his office. Before long he returned, announcing that I couldn't get any money, and worse, that he'd have to keep my card. When I asked why, he told me that the bank that issued my card had requested that he retain it.

I was confused. I was in good standing. The young rep and I went back and forth until I requested a meeting with his manager.

"He'll tell you the same thing that I've been telling you," he said as he curtly dismissed me.

I repeatedly insisted that he get his manager. The rep huffed and puffed his way to the boss's office to resentfully convey my message.

Mike asked me what the problem was. I assured him there must be a mistake and that it would all be cleared up shortly. His face filled with "My dad can handle it" confidence. After waiting for nearly ten minutes, I caught the service rep and a man I took to be the manager in my peripheral vision as they headed to an empty desk. The manager opened the drawer and pulled out a pair of scissors. The blood began to boil in my veins. Those scissors could only mean one thing: he was going to cut my card in two, and with it, my dignity. The manager hadn't had the decency or respect to speak to me directly before obviously choosing to take action.

"Sir, if you're about to do what I fear you will, can we please talk first?"

Of course he ignored me and sliced my card in half before what had now become a considerable crowd. I bolted from my seat and followed him as he walked off without speaking to me. Mike trailed close behind me, crying, tearfully asking me over and over again, "Daddy, what's going on?"

I hurried into the manager's office and begged him for privacy to spare me further embarrassment.

"Don't let him close the door," the manager barked as he waved three other employees into his office. He wasn't going to face the angry black man alone, a man who was only angry because he had not been treated with respect.

I snatched the pieces of my card from his hands. I told him I was a reputable member of the community. I told him I was a good customer of his bank. I said that had I been wearing a three-piece suit, and not the black running suit I had on, and had I been a white man, he would have at least spoken to me in private. He would have spared me the humiliation of having what felt like my manhood snipped before a leering crowd of onlookers who saw only an enraged and deflated black man. I insisted that a mistake had been made and that my bill had been paid.

The manager showed no sympathy. His face was flushed. He pointed his index finger beneath his desk drawer and pushed a button.

"I'm calling the police on you."

I became even angrier. I fantasized about venting my spleen on his pasty face. I sped through the likely scenario in my mind. I would lunge at his neck. His coworkers would join the melee. They'd all attack me and maybe hurt my son.

That calmed me down. I knew that if I stayed it was likely the police wouldn't hear me either and I'd only end up arrested in front of my son, leaving him even more mortified than he was already. I grabbed Mike's hand and beat a hasty retreat right as the police were pulling up.

Later, I made several phone calls. The bank's board eventually apologized to me and issued me a new MasterCard. But the incident reminded me yet again that no matter how much Ivy League education I had, I was still a *nigger* in the eyes of many white folk.

✤   ✤   ✤

Beloved, to be black in America is to live in terror. That terror is fast. It is glimpsed in cops giving chase to black men and shooting them in their backs without cause. Or the terror is slow. It chips like lead paint on a tenement wall, or flows like contaminated water through corroded pipes that poison black bodies. It is slow like genocide inside prison walls where folk who should not be there perish.

Maybe the reason you can't feel our terror is because you don't live in our skin. Our skin, our bodies, are relentlessly monitored and policed. Our skin bleeds the secret of our fear in scrapes with law enforcement's view of "broken windows." We endure the terror of being stopped and frisked and sent to jail for possessing less than an ounce of weed that the cops discovered while looking for someone who stole beer and "fit our description." But they all fit our description—black and breathing—at least at the beginning of the encounter.

We think of the police who kill us for no good reason as ISIS. That shouldn't surprise you. Cops rain down terror on our heads with relentless fire and make us afraid to walk the streets. At any moment, without warning, a blue-clad monster will swoop down on us to snatch our lives from us and say that it was because we were selling cigarettes, or compact discs, or breathing too much for his comfort, or speaking too abrasively for his taste. Or running, or standing still, or talking back, or being silent, or doing as you say, or not doing as you say fast enough.

Like all terrorists they hate us for who we are. They hate us because of the bad things they—and you—think we do. Like breathe. Live. That is our sin. Death is our only redemption. You do not condemn these cops. To do so, you would have to condemn the culture of whiteness that produced them—that produced you. Racial terror is not just an act, but a habit, not luck, but a skill, a genius for snuffing out black life over mundane things—a wallet, some candy, loud music, a cell phone, a toy gun, shopping, the failure to signal, or other minor offenses that white people live to tell us about when they commit them.

It is easy for you to be oblivious to what black people must remember. Memory is survival, and everything about us, around us, on us, even our cells, remembers. Even bodies wrapped in Sunday dress or business wear can't really mask the memory. Our children cloak their bodies in over-size clothing to smother the hate that might one day suffo-cate them. Our jewelry is a talisman to ward off the evil that might roll up on us when we aren't looking. We know that it is hard to run from what we can't see coming our way and we never want to be caught off guard by your fatal whimsy. We don't know how or when one of you might pounce. You might be dressed in bright, well-pressed, angry blue with shining accessories meant to club or kill us. Or you might snuff us wearing the jersey of a star who was once a poor black boy who made it all the way from the ghetto to your fantasy. You don't think of him as black. You think of us as nothing else but black. It is a blackness you despise or fear or resent or simply don't understand or care to know. And that difference is the margin of life and death for us.

Dear Gentle White Listener, do you want to know the harsh realities of which I speak? Then let me take you on a brief Tour of Terror.

✢   ✢   ✢

Beloved, you must understand that for us terror pulses in the body of the cop. The police come loaded with far bigger weapons than they carry on their hips. The heat they pack is drawn from history. It's all there next to their badges and guns and their Tasers and mace. Spreading state-sanctioned violence. Menacing black communities. Seeing blackness as criminal. Punishing back talk. Killing blacks who run.

The policeman has never been neutral to us. From the start he was not there to protect or serve us, but to protect and serve you, which often meant getting rid of us. The policing of the black body started in slavery when enslaved men and women had handcuffs slapped on their wrists and irons fixed on their legs as they got jammed into the hulls of slave ships.

The nation got up slave patrols to bring back the enslaved who ran away—to stop, question, and frisk them, just like many of us are treated today, to monitor, search, and arrest them, to beat them down when they were recaptured. Free Africans weren't so free. As many of you learned by watching *12 Years a Slave,* free Africans were routinely tracked by bounty hunters and sold into slavery. The line between enslaved and free was never sure, and the word of a free African meant little in a southern court when pitted against the claims of white bounty hunters. When slavery ended, the slave patrols ceased, but the need to police black space did not, so the Klan and police squads rose up in their place. The rapper KRS-One drew a direct line from the plantation to postindustrial urban America phonetically when he pronounced "overseer" as "officer."

In the fifties and sixties, many local police officers swore by white supremacy, and some even secretly joined the Klan to terrorize and kill black folk. The Klan was legal, but, still, officers of the law shouldn't join a white terrorist organization to illegally kill black folk. Jimmie Lee Jackson was a black, unarmed Vietnam War veteran whose murder in a café by white Alabama State trooper James Bonard Fowler in 1965 helped to inspire the Selma to Montgomery marches. It was not until 42 years later in 2007 that Fowler was finally charged with homicide in Jackson's death, pleading guilty to one count of second-degree manslaughter and serving five months of a six-month sentence. When Fowler shot him, Jackson managed to flee the café, but was clubbed by other state troopers before he was eventually taken to a hospital where he died eight days later. Jackson relayed the story of his shooting and beating to his lawyer, Oscar Adams, in the hospital in the presence of FBI agents. The FBI often dragged their feet on official civil rights investigations and suppressed information about assassination plots against movement leaders like Martin Luther King, Jr., who referred in his "I Have a Dream" speech to the "unspeakable horrors of police brutality."

Since the seventies the police have battled efforts to integrate their forces so that they would reflect the communities they serve. They have often been a vicious occupying force in our neighborhoods. White cops have frequently tried out their racist talk and ugly behavior on black and brown officers before assaulting the broader community. When politicians talk of restoring trust between black folk and the cops, they are seriously deluded, or they have a gigantic case of amnesia. Black and brown folk have never trusted the cops.

You cannot know the terror that black folk feel when a cop car makes its approach and the history of racism and violence comes crashing down on us. The police car is a mobile plantation, and the siren is the sound of dogs hunting us down in the dark woods.

My friends, please don't pretend you can't understand how we feel this way. And if you claim that slavery and Jim Crow and the sixties are ancient history, you know your words are lies before they leave your lips. How could that history be erased so quickly?

How can all of that be got rid of overnight? How can it be washed, without great effort, from the mind of a white cop who confronts black folk? How can we deny the structures, systems, and social forces that shape how black folk are seen and treated?

Beloved, the way we feel about cops is how many of you feel in the face of terror. And yet, long before 9/11, long before Al-Qaeda, long before ISIS, we felt that too, at your hands, at the hands of your ancestors, at the hands of your kin who are our cops.

(Do you ever thank your lucky stars that black folk have not done to you what terrorists who despise this country have done? These terrorists claim their actions are driven by hate for our nation. Does it ever give you pause and make you say, "Thank God that black folk never—well, almost never—poisoned our food when we made them cook for us. They never killed our children when we made them watch over them. They rarely conspired to murder us in our sleep when we forced them to share intimate space with us. They never rose up in unison against us because we raped their women, murdered their children, and castrated their men." Does that ever cross your minds?)

You cannot know how we secretly curse the cowardice of whites who know what I write is true, but dare not say it. Neither will your smug dismissal of unenlightened and bigoted whites satisfy us any longer. That they're "poor white trash" or uncouth rednecks and that you're better than they are, that they don't have your social pedigree or education.

As if you can really separate yourselves from them. As if it's only a matter of personal belief and not social learning and behavior. The distinction between them and you is more self-serving than critical. In the end it only makes the slaughter of our people worse to know that your disapproval of those white folk has spared your reputations but not our lives.

You do not know that after we get angry with you, we get even angrier with ourselves, because we don't really know how to make you stop.

Do you really think that black people bring this terror upon ourselves? That a woman who's being intimidated by a cop and calls 911 brings it on herself? How absurd is it to have to call the cops on the cops and then have the cop get mad and not be disciplined or punished? How absurd is it that not a single cop got held accountable for Freddie Gray's death, as if he somehow snapped his own spine to spite the Baltimore police?

Most of you say nothing, and your silence is not only deafening, it is defeating. And when there is white response, it is often white noise, inane chatter accompanied by the wringing of white hands. There is white frustration at just how complex the problem is and how hard it is for you to tell from the angles of the video just what went down.

Most of us keep our rage inside. We are afraid that when those tears begin to flow we cannot stop them. Instead we damage our insides with high blood pressure, worry our minds with mental distress, or sicken our souls with depression. We pray to God for our sanity. Yet the aggression buried deep inside us sometimes blocks our belief and makes us functional atheists.

✝ ✝ ✝

Part of our problem, beloved, is that the police bring overwhelming credibility and authority to the table. Our troubles are worsened when politicians insist that cops and unarmed black folk are equal. Police have badges and batons and Tasers and bullets and guns. Police begin with a shield of honor and incorruptibility. Police start with the support of the state.

We are hardly equal.

Police start with the belief that we must protect our cops as if the history of racial terror doesn't exist. Police seem to believe they possess what we might term *copistemology,* or unquestionable knowledge of black guilt and moral blasphemy. There is no need to prove it in court. The streets are where their knowledge is tested as they answer with a billy club or a bullet. Copistemology apparently works wonders. It lets cops know when they should break into the home of a mentally challenged black woman and fatally shoot her while she cradles a child and a shotgun. (But there seem to be gaps in cops' knowledge too. They didn't know that the same woman blamed the police for a miscarriage she experienced after an earlier arrest.)

Cops seem to know when to shoot and kill a mentally disturbed black woman as her child watched from the backseat *after* she changed her mind and drove away from the White House and posed a mortal threat to no one. Cops always seem to know that the black person who is eccentric, or mentally deranged, deserves to die. Yet they also seem to know that the demented white bigot who mows down nine black folk in a southern church deserves to be treated to fast food before being calmly booked. Cops seem to know that all those white folk who come at cops with swinging fists or menacing demeanors or drawn guns don't really mean them any harm.

Beloved, surely you must see that cops loathe being held accountable for their actions, especially when it comes to us. The cops and their advocates claim that only a few rogue cops give a bad name to the rest. But isn't that like claiming that most of one's cells are healthy and that only a few are cancerous?

That metaphor of a few bad apples doesn't begin to get at the root of the problem. Police violence may be more like a poisoned water stream that pollutes the entire system. To argue that only a few bad cops cause police terror is like relegating racism to a few bigots. Bigots are surely a problem, but they are sustained by systems of belief and perception, by widely held stereotypes and social practice.

Cops are human, they tell us. They are right. That also means that cops cannot possibly be immune to the destructive beliefs about black folk. Their fear and suspicion of black folk doesn't come from nowhere. It materializes the cumulative history of injustice toward black folk. That history gets reduced to intuition about any black person and their likelihood of presenting a threat to the cop's life. Some "I feared for my life" testimony is pure hogwash. It is the cop's attempt, after the fact, to justify his criminal actions. But it is just as lethal when the cop honestly believes that he is in danger just by being in the presence of a black person, no matter how much the objective circumstances suggest otherwise.

To pretend that the solution is to bring back a lost balance between black folk and cops ignores history, ignores racial terror, ignores how things are not, and have never been, equal. It is to ignore the even more insistent strains of *Coptopia,* an ideal state of affairs where police can display ghastly inventiveness in traumatizing or disappearing black and brown bodies while demanding even greater public reverence.

✦   ✦   ✦

The myths and demands of Coptopia flare when there is an egregious crime against the police, like the assassination of officers in Dallas and Baton Rouge. In both cities a young black man took aim at the cops through his hateful crosshairs and cut down innocent public servants. Both men expressed their outrage at law enforcement's seeming war on vulnerable and innocent black folk. The vast majority of black people sided with the police and not the men whose twisted actions spilled innocent blood.

Yet in each case the advocates of Coptopia insisted on complete empathy with the cops' outlook. They also sought to erase the long and vile history of police terror. They insisted that Black Lives Matter was racist and a spur to violence against cops, even though BLM spoke out immediately against each man's actions. Neither of these poisonous young assassins was nurtured in a black movement. They were products of our military. Each was taught to use lethal force in the service of his country. These veterans may have both suffered from PTSD. Imagine if every time a white person committed a crime, especially a mass shooting, all white people had to apologize.

Beloved, you should be honest even when it hurts to do so. It is little wonder that these men twisted their anger at the terror black folk face into a perverted plot to murder innocent cops. The real wonder is that more black folk haven't gone berserk like these men did.

The moral courage of the black masses is overlooked at such moments of crisis. But then how could white America acknowledge our moral courage? It would undercut the rationale for terror that we have faced all along. It would mean that your society, your culture, are culprits in a racial terror that is far more damaging than political terror. The terror we face at your hands is far more sustained. The terror we experience has claimed millions more lives over the long haul of history.

A conservative white commentator bravely pointed out what many of you fail to see. In looking at the forces that might have provoked the evil in Dallas, Leon H. Wolf argued that there's "a reality that we don't often talk about—that societies are held together less by laws and force and threats of force than we are by ethereal and fragile concepts like mutual respect and belief in the justness of the system itself."

That compact has obviously been shattered for blacks. Wolf said it is impossible for the police to do their jobs without the vast majority of citizens believing that our society is basically just and that the police are there to protect them. Wolf asked us to imagine what might happen if a subcommunity perceived that those bonds had dissolved in application to them. We are products of the way our parents view society and institutions, and that, in turn, shapes how we view the world, something we don't often acknowledge. Beloved, that "we" is really "you."

Most black folk get this point. We have been arguing it until we were blue in the face. Wolf admitted that as the child of white parents in rural Texas, he was taught the police were there to help him at any time and that he should follow their orders and show great respect for them. Wolf asked white folk to imagine that their parents were black and had grown up in the fifties or sixties in areas where the police force was an instrument of oppression. He asked how that might understandably change those folks' interactions with the police, and their children's children's interactions too, and how it might affect their belief that the police can be held accountable for abusing their power.

Wolf delivered a tough reflection on the events in Dallas. He said that, in order to prevent what happened in Dallas, we must bolster the belief that when cops commit crimes, that the legal system "will punish them accordingly." Wolf said that if minority communities could believe that this was the case, then there'd be little to no perceived need for reprisal killings.

Wolf acknowledged that "a huge, overwhelming segment of America does not really give a damn what cops do in the course of maintaining order because they assume (probably correctly) that abuse at the hands of the police will never happen to them. As long as the cops keep people away from my door, they have my blessing handling 'the thugs' in whatever way they see fit."

Notice, beloved, that Wolf didn't take easy refuge in the highly questionable 2016 study—cited in the *New York Times* and many other media outlets—authored by Harvard professor Roland Fryer, that concluded that black folk are less likely to be shot in a conflict with the police than suspects of other races. The study was doomed by a few factors. First, it only studied ten police departments in three states. It also underplayed the widely varying institutional frameworks that shape how policing is done from department to department. The three states Fryer examined are all members of a White House initiative on policing data that got started in 2015, suggesting that a measure of self-selection, self-fulfillment is at play: departments that already value data-collection and transparency will have different outcomes in any such study because of their laudatory priorities.

It quickly becomes clear that there simply wasn't enough data in Fryer's study. Compare the amount of information in Fryer's study to that of the FBI's Uniform Crime Report database, which collects data from thousands of police departments across the land. The data Fryer studied in three states over 16 years is about equal to what the FBI database is able to collect in just two to three years. To quote the philosopher Shawn Carter, "We don't believe you, you need more people." Fryer concluded that there's scant statistical difference between the races when the police stop them. But the basis for his conclusion is troubling. Fryer studied folk who had already been stopped by the police, and were then subsequently killed. He never asks—plain avoids—the question of whether black folk are more likely to be stopped in the first place, and whether they're more likely to be stopped for no good reason.

The answer to both questions is yes. A serious flaw riddled Fryer's data: it did not distinguish between the likelihood of getting shot when being accosted by police for a traffic infraction or for shooting up a church—only the likelihood of getting shot. As noted journalist Dara Lind cogently argues, "When people talk about racial disparities in police use of force, they're usually not asking, *Is a black American stopped by police treated the same as a white American in the same circumstances?* . . . They're saying that black Americans are more likely to get stopped by police, which makes them more likely to get killed."

✣   ✣   ✣

Beloved, surely you understand how vexed we are by our situation. Surely you understand how the legacy of terror stalks us at every turn, dogs our every step. Surely you understand that police brutality pounds our lives in unrelenting waves. Can you not see that too many cops kill us off like animals without a second thought?

For God's sake, imagine little Johnny being executed because he drank too much liquor and mouthed off at the cops. Imagine little Jill getting her long blonde hair yanked and her arms pulled behind her back and being slapped around and beat down because she dared ask why

she was being stopped. Or being thrown around her classroom because she didn't want to give up her phone. Imagine seeing video of cops high-fiving each other after one of
them heartlessly shoots down your unarmed buddy Larry
for no good reason. Imagine hearing one cop whisper to
a fellow cop that he should make sure his body camera is
turned off.

Beloved, you must not be defensive when you hear our
hurt. We who proclaim the terror of cops do not hate all
cops. We hate what cops have been made to be. We hate
how cops hate us. We hate that cops don't treat us the way
they treat you.

And we hate that you won't deal with the elephant in
the room. Black and brown cops have been the victims of
racism themselves. They are the guinea pigs of racism on a
police force they are often seduced, or coerced, into lying
for. Black police often face harsher barriers to promotion.
They often witness firsthand the vile bigotry of white police
officers but are afraid to report those officers for fear of a
blue backlash. Or think of Ohio black police officer Nakia
Jones, who caused a firestorm of controversy for telling the
truth about how some white cops target black folk for mayhem. "So why don't we just keep it real: If you are that officer
that knows good and well you've got a god complex . . . you
are afraid of people who don't look like you—you have no
business in that uniform," Jones said on a Facebook video.
"You have no business being a police officer . . . If you are
that officer that's prejudiced, take that uniform off and put
a KKK hoodie on." Cops like Jones are either isolated or
silenced. We hate that too.

We hate that body cameras seem to make no real difference, and police often refuse to share the footage. We hate that the folk who share the videos of the cops killing us are often harassed. Chris LeDay, a 34-year-old Atlanta Air Force veteran, didn't film, but he did post the video of Alton Sterling, a husband and father of five, being shot by a cop outside of a Louisiana convenience store in July 2016. The next day, military security detained LeDay at his job on Dobbins Air Reserve Base as he passed through a routine checkpoint. He was initially told he fit the description of a black man wanted for assault and battery. It was only after he was taken in handcuffs and leg shackles to DeKalb County jail that he learned that he faced a charge of "failure to appear" on an unpaid traffic ticket from 2014. We hate that you do this.

We hate that you won't admit that if your children or kin were being killed like us you wouldn't turn your heads or avert your eyes or accept it as business as usual or the price we must pay to keep our society safe. You'd be beside yourself if your children were slaughtered, and then had their slaughter justified on television, and on social media, as their names were heedlessly dragged through the mud because they playfully posed as a gangsta and posted the photo to their Facebook or Twitter account. How many of your kids do that too? Yet they grow up to be bankers and lawyers or cops who kill black people because those black people provoke suspicion by doing the very thing those same cops did when they were young. But they didn't end up dead. They end up making us dead. We hate that.

Beloved, one thing is clear: until we confront the terror that black folk have faced in this country from the time
we first breathed American air, we will continue to die at
the hands of cops whose whiteness is far more important in
explaining their behavior than the dangerous circumstances
they face and the impossible choices they confront.

We do not hate you, white America. We hate that you
terrorize us and then lie about it and then make us feel crazy
for having to explain to you how crazy it makes us feel. We
cannot hate you, not really, not most of us; that is our gift
to you. We cannot halt you; that is our curse.

VI.

BENEDICTION

R.E.S.P.O.N.S.I.V.E.

This old man was very wise, and he could answer questions that was almost impossible for people to answer. So some people went to him one day, two young people, and said, "We're going to trick this guy today. We're going to catch a bird, and we're going to carry it to this old man. And we're going to ask him, 'This that we hold in our hands today, is it alive or is it dead?' If he says 'Dead,' we're going to turn it loose and let it fly. But if he says, 'Alive,' we're going to crush it." So they walked up to this old man, and they said, "This that we hold in our hands today, is it alive or is it dead?" He looked at the young people and he smiled. And he said, "It's in your hands."

—Fannie Lou Hamer

Beloved, in this sermon I have shared with you from the depths of my heart what I believe to be true about the state of race in America. As we prepare to part, I offer you a few practical suggestions about what you as individuals can do to make things better.

First, my friends, you must make *reparation*. I know that you may not have followed the fierce debate over reparations, and even if you have, you may not support the idea. If affirmative action is a hard sell for many of you, then reparations, the notion that the descendants of enslaved Africans should receive from the society that exploited them some form of compensation, is beyond the pale. But surely you can see the justice of making reparation, even if you can't make it happen politically. Please don't say that your ancestors didn't own slaves. Your white privilege has not been hampered by that fact. Black sweat built the country you now reside in, and you continue to enjoy the fruits of that labor.

There are all sorts of ways to make reparation work at the local and individual level. You can hire black folk at your office and pay them slightly better than you would ordinarily pay them. You can pay the black person who cuts your grass double what you might ordinarily pay. Or you can give a deserving black student in your neighborhood, or one you run across in the course of your work, scholarship help. In fact, your religious or civic institution can commit a tenth of its resources to educating black youth.

It may be best to think of reparation as a secular tithe, a proportion of money and other resources set aside for causes that are worthy of support. You can, as an individual or as a small group, set up an I.R.A., an Individual Reparations Account. There are thousands upon thousands of black kids whose parents cannot afford to send them to summer camp or to pay fees for a sports team, or to buy instruments to play if they attend one of the ever-shrinking number of schools that has a band. Their parents cannot pay for tutors for math or science or English or whatever subject their kids need help with. An I.R.A. would work just fine.

You can also pay a black tax, just as black folk do. The black tax refers to the cost and penalty of being black in America—of having to work twice as hard for half of what whites get by less strenuous means. You can help defray the black tax by offering black tax incentives: if a black accountant is doing a good job for you, assume a surcharge and pay her more. If a black lawyer performs good service, then compensate him even more for his labor.

You can also treat some black folk to a few of the signs of appreciation you offer to military veterans. For instance, at football games, there ought to be a "civil rights veterans" night to recognize the valor, honor, and sacrifice of those who made this country great—living legends like Andrew Young, Diane Nash, Jesse Jackson, John Lewis, and Eleanor Holmes Norton.

As part of an I.R.A. you can also pay for massages for working class folk. You can choose five black children to sponsor on an annual trip to the local zoo. You can begin a film club for black children to attend movie theaters in more affluent areas where they might also enjoy a trip to the museum. Or you can pay for the textbooks of ten black college students each year. The point is to be creative in transferring a bit of your resources, even if in modest amounts, to deserving and often struggling descendants of the folk who gave this country its great wealth and whose offspring rescued its reputation for democracy.

Beloved, you must also *educate* yourselves about black life and culture. Racial literacy is as necessary as it is undervalued.

What should you read? I always start with James Baldwin, the most ruthlessly honest analyst of white innocence yet to pick up a pen. Baldwin was a boy preacher, and though he outgrew the rituals and theology that hemmed in the very souls religion meant to free, he never left the pulpit. His words drip with the searing eloquence of an evangelist of race determined to get to the brutal bottom of America's original sin. Baldwin married the gospel fervor of Jonathan Edwards to the literary style of Henry James, most notably in *The Fire Next Time.*

Beloved, you should read books about slavery that prove it was far more varied and complicated than once believed, including Ira Berlin's incisive history of slavery before cotton became king in *Many Thousands Gone;* Stephanie Camp's *Closer to Freedom,* which explores the fate of enslaved women; and books like Thavolia Glymph's *Out of the House of Bondage,* which probes the relationships between black and white women. The novels *The Known World,* by Edward P. Jones, about a black family that owned enslaved blacks in the antebellum south, and Charles Johnson's *Middle Passage,* about a newly freed slave who hops aboard a slave ship, give color and texture to slavery. Toni Morrison's epic novel *Beloved* lyrically probes the aftereffects of enslavement on the minds and souls of black folk. Her *Playing in the Dark* is a slim classic that brilliantly probes the white literary imagination and how it silences and distorts the dark agency from which it derives its meaning.

Slavery was ensconced in politics, intertwined with the economy, and thus you need to know impressive works like Steven Hahn's *A Nation Under Our Feet,* Manisha Sinha's *The Counterrevolution of Slavery,* Walter Johnson's *Soul by Soul,* Sven Beckert's *Empire of Cotton,* and Edward E. Baptist's *The Half Has Never Been Told.* Vincent Brown's *The Reaper's Garden* offers a haunting glimpse into what enslaved, and enslaving, people in the Atlantic world made of death. Drew Gilpin Faust's *This Republic of Suffering* does for the Civil War what Brown does for slavery. The Civil War was, centrally, the infernal contest of white regions over black flesh and its future in America, which you'll discover when you tackle James McPherson's fiercely elegant *Battle Cry of Freedom.* You should read about what went on after the Civil War, especially classics like W.E.B. Du Bois' *Black Reconstruction in America* and Eric Foner's *Reconstruction.* And you should ride the epic sweep of black migration along with Isabel Wilkerson in her achingly brilliant *The Warmth of Other Suns.*

Beloved, take in as much as you can about the modern civil rights movement, glimpsed in stellar works like Aldon Morris' *Origins of the Civil Rights Movement* and Henry Hampton and Steve Fayer's *Voices of Freedom,* the book based on Hampton's monumental documentary television series *Eyes on the Prize,* which you should make every effort to see. Or you can make your way through Taylor Branch's trilogy on Martin Luther King, Jr., and the civil rights movement, in *Parting the Waters, Pillar of Fire,* and *At Canaan's Edge*—or the single-volume summary *America in the King Years*—and David Garrow's exhaustive and illuminating study of King, *Bearing the Cross,* or Diane McWhorter's riveting account of the movement's impact on white families in Birmingham, including her own, in *Carry Me Home.* Gilbert King's heartbreaking *Devil in the Grove* shines a light on Jim Crow as he probes the case of four young black men accused of raping a 17-year-old white girl in Florida and the valiant defense they got from future Supreme Court justice Thurgood Marshall. You should also read Barbara Ransby's moving portrait of the great organizer and activist, *Ella Baker and the Black Freedom Movement;* Kay Mills' engrossing study of freedom fighter Fannie Lou Hamer, *This Little Light of Mine;* and *In Struggle,* Clayborne Carson's compelling study of the Student Nonviolent Coordinating Committee.

Grapple with the black freedom struggle, too, especially the impact of black nationalism's most influential leader, Malcolm X, explored in Manning Marable's magnum opus *Malcolm X.* Peniel Joseph's seminal *Waiting 'Til the Midnight Hour* invites us to understand the rich sweep of the black power movement, as does his penetrating study of the movement's most iconic leader, Stokely Carmichael, in his biography *Stokely.* To understand how the issue of police brutality inspired social revolution in the seventies, please read *Black against Empire,* a comprehensive study of the history and politics of the Black Panthers by Joshua Bloom and Waldo Martin, Jr. The struggle of black working class folk is captured in Robin Kelley's landmark *Race Rebels.* The effort to embrace the intersections of gender, class, sexuality, and feminist politics is portrayed in a series of pioneering books, including Audre Lorde's *Sister Outsider,* Barbara Smith's *The Truth That Never Hurts,* bell hooks' *Ain't I a Woman?,* Michele Wallace's *Black Macho and the Myth of the Superwoman,* Kimberlé Crenshaw's *Critical Race Theory* and, along with co-author Andrea Ritchie, *Say Her Name,* and Patricia Hill Collins' *Black Feminist Thought.*

Beloved, these are just a few books to get you started. Of course the classics must not be neglected, from Du Bois' *The Souls of Black Folk,* groundbreaking essays that limn the color line at the turn of the twentieth century, to Ralph Ellison's novel *Invisible Man,* which wrestles with the perennial black problem of not being seen by the white world. Ellison's collected essays are masterpieces of elegance and erudition. And you should pay attention to the personal and political essays of LeRoi Jones/Amiri Baraka; June Jordan; Zora Neale Hurston (and her great novel rejecting racial uplift narratives, *Their Eyes Were Watching God*); and the essays of Alice Walker, along with *The Color Purple,* her captivating novel about the struggles of black women for room to breathe and love in the south in the 1930s. Great black autobiographies offer a peek into the struggles of some of our most important figures, from *Narrative of the Life of Frederick Douglass* to Booker T. Washington's *Up from Slavery,* from *The Autobiography of Malcolm X* to *Angela Davis: An*

Autobiography, and from Maya Angelou's *I Know Why the Caged Bird Sings* to Barack Obama's *Dreams from My Father.*

Beloved, you should read as much as you can about race and black identity in the media too. Read gifted black voices like Jamilah Lemieux, Ta-Nehisi Coates, William Jelani Cobb, Jamelle Bouie, Eve Ewing, Clint Smith, Wesley Lowery, Damon Young, Vann Newkirk, Mychal Denzel Smith, Bakari Kitwana, Rembert Browne, Wesley Morris, Nicole Hannah-Jones, and Keisha Blain. The miracle of social media permits greater accessibility than in the past to brilliant thinkers and scholars like Henry Louis Gates, Jr.; Mark Anthony Neal; Marc Lamont Hill; James Braxton Peterson; Salamishah Tillet; Stacey Patton; Kiese Laymon; Melissa Harris-Perry; Treva Lindsey; Obery Hendricks, Jr.; Farah Griffin; Brittney Cooper; Stacy Floyd-Thomas; Elizabeth Hinton; Alondra Nelson; Thadious Davis; Tracy Denean Sharpley-Whiting; Keri Day; Eboni Marshall Turman; Lawrence Bobo; Leah Wright Rigueur; Marcylinena Morgan; Nell Painter; and thousands more.

Beloved, you must not only read about black life, but you must **school** your white brothers and sisters, your cousins and uncles, your loved ones and friends, and all who will listen to you, about the white elephant in the room— white privilege. Share with them what you learn about us, but share as well what you learn about yourself, about how whiteness works. You see, my friends, there is only so much I can say to white folk, only so much they can hear from me or anyone who isn't white. They may not be as defensive with you, so you must be an ambassador of truth to your own tribes, just like the writers Peggy McIntosh, Tim

Wise, David Roediger, Mab Segrest, Theodore Allen, and
Joe Feagin.

It is your obligation, beloved, to school yourselves, and
other white folk, too, about the seductive, mythical, neutrality of whiteness, the belief that you are somehow American
without a racial identity, without racial baggage. "While it is
dangerous to say that all whites have equal access to wealth
and education," one of my white students writes, "the fact
of the matter is that white people will not be followed in a
store, frisked on a New York sidewalk, or shot by police at
the same rate as black people. Whites must understand that
they benefit from white privilege in order to realize how
white privilege creates the space for black oppression."

You see what my student did there, beloved? He linked
white privilege and black oppression, not directly, mind
you, but in a way that suggests that white privilege creates
opportunities for black oppression to take hold. If white folk
refuse to name white privilege for what it is, then it is more
likely that you will ignore how black inequality, black suffering, exists all around you. Those of you who know better
than that must tell other white people what you know. As
one of my students says, "if one stays silent" then one is "actually helping racial injustice persist." Beloved, racism and
bigotry are ugly, uncomfortable issues to grapple with. But
if you don't address them, you reinforce the privilege of not
having to face up to the truth.

Beloved, your ***participation*** in protests, rallies, local
community meetings, and the like makes a huge difference.
When we gather to express grief, outrage, and dissent, your
presence sends the signal that this is not "just a black thing."

It is, instead, an American thing. Your white bodies don't just desegregate the images that communicate social concern. Your presence also puts your bodies and reputations on the line by identifying you with folk you are not supposed to have much in common with. Your presence adds greater moral weight to the gathering. It shouldn't have to be that way, but for now, it is.

My friends, I know that there is a valiant, even volatile, history of white participation in black struggles for freedom. And some of your mothers and fathers, and your grandmothers and grandfathers, too, got their feelings hurt when black folk told them their help was no longer needed. This was the case in the sixties when black folk were coming into our own and younger black folk in more radical organizations wanted to feel their own power, take further charge of their own destinies. Surely you know that white participation doesn't mean white takeover.

You must grapple with how your participation isn't just to aid black and brown folk, though that is indeed admirable. It is also to fulfill your sense of destiny. One of your great prophets, Jim Wallis, the founder and leader of the Washington, D.C.–based Christian community called Sojourners, hammered this home recently. Wallis quotes black theologian James Cone who "talks about 'repentance for white people as dying to whiteness.' I want to say white Christians have been separated from God by the idolatry of whiteness. So we're not in this to help somebody else. We're in this for our own souls."

Wallis' point underscores a vital need, my friends, the need to close the distance between the white self and the

black *other*. In fact, viewing black folk—or brown folk, or
gay folk, or poor folk—as the other is the problem. This
country has just lived through the first black presidency in
our nation's history. Whether one liked or loathed Barack
Obama's politics, there is no denying that he is one of the
most profound, impressive, gifted, and inspiring Americans
this nation has seen in quite some time. And yet there was
a relentless attempt to make him the "other." The collective
effort to deprive Obama of his legitimacy, of his citizenship,
of his humanity, scarred the body politic and did great damage to our efforts to move this country beyond its heinous
racial history.

In your own lives, at your own jobs, in your own communities—and in your own minds—you must see and
root out and oppose how black folk are routinely made
the cultural other. You must resist the impulse to see black
schoolchildren as the educational other. You must fight the
inclination to dismiss black coworkers as the other because
of their hairstyles, their dress, their speech, their demeanors.
You must constantly ask yourselves how you are thinking
of, and responding to, the black folk you encounter in ordinary venues. When you are interviewing black folk for
jobs, for fellowships, for positions in your service, are you
seeing them as incapable of learning and adapting just as
white folk do? The dismissal of black and brown folk in
this manner, often unconsciously, scars them with missed
opportunity and denied humanity.

Not knowing black folk intimately exacerbates the
distance between the white self and the black other. One
solution is *new* black friends. It is distressing that so few

of you have more than a token black friend, maybe two. Every open-minded white person should set out immediately to find and make friends with black folk who share their interests. It's not as hard as it seems. Black folk come in every variety of belief, ideology, and politics, just as any other American does, and the vast majority of us are morally upright.

Honestly, the fact that you do not know real, ordinary, splendid black folk is astonishing. The more black folk you know, the less likely you are to stereotype us. The less you stereotype us, the less likely you are to fear us. The less you fear us, the less likely you are to want to hurt us, or to accept our hurt as the price of your safekeeping. The safer you feel, the safer we'll be.

Beloved, hopefully your new friends will make it easier for you to *speak up* against the injustice that black folk face. Martin Luther King, Jr., said that we would have to repent not only for the "evil words and deeds of the bad people, but for the appalling silence of the good people." We need to hear your voices ring out against our suffering loud and clear.

When a black or brown youth is railroaded in a court system for possessing a negligible amount of marijuana, it makes a difference if a sea of white witnesses floods the airways, or cyberspace, or community halls, or prosecutors' offices, or congressional staff with e-mails, letters, speeches, and commentary about the injustice of such acts. If white folk take to social media and testify to how they got away with the very minor offenses that cause black and brown folk trouble—that cause our kids to be sent to jail or prison—it might move the needle of awareness and set change in motion. If honest white voices speak up about how your own children are not expelled at the same rates as black and brown kids for the same offenses, it will put pressure on local school boards to reconsider their unjust policies and practices.

When there are traumatic public events that the world can see, we need clear white voices of resistance that the world can hear.

Beloved, your voices are crucial because the doubt of black humanity, the skepticism of black intelligence, and the denial of the worth of black bodies linger in our cultural unconscious and shadow our national politics. If you challenge white ignorance, or indifference, to the plight of people of color, it will lend our cause needed legitimacy.

One of the issues about which you might speak, especially in your own circles, is the distinction between the *immigrant* and black American experiences. Of course those experiences overlap; we often forget that black folk who hail from the Caribbean or from Africa come to America seeking opportunity like any other immigrants. I have in mind the argument that black folk should do like the European immigrants who came to America and worked hard to become successful. The best response to such a baseless comparison is a direct one: whiteness matters. My friends, in the short term, and in the long run, too, being Irish, or Italian, or Polish, or Jewish hasn't been as large a deficit to achievement as color has been for black folk. It is true that the barriers of language, ethnicity, and culture are big ones, but they don't make the same difference that being black makes.

White immigrants came to this country, and still do, with white skin, the biggest asset possible in a country where whiteness still has tremendous value. It makes no sense to tell black folk to do what white immigrants did to become successful.

My friends, if whiteness matters, slavery does too. The legacy of inequality is both formal and informal, both a matter of law and a matter of social convention. European immigrants certainly faced their own barriers to assimilation. But neither the government nor our society used its legal and political power to stop immigrant success the way America did to stop black folk for nearly three centuries.

Black immigrants often have a leg up on American blacks as well. They have arrived from societies where they enjoyed equality without regard to color. Thus they arrive with great assets, skills, and experiences, allowing them to compete in the American marketplace. These black immigrants faced no color barriers to human capital like those we face in America. Neither can we discount the exotic appeal of foreign blackness. Many white folk find it far more attractive to deal with a black person from the Caribbean or Africa than American blacks. Foreign blacks lack the common history of oppression that binds black Americans together. That difference is a big one for white folk. You don't feel the sort of pressure of history when you encounter many of those immigrant blacks. Neither do you feel the sort of white racial guilt you may experience in the presence of American blacks. If you do a good enough job of reading up on the black experience, you can fight those arguments in your own circles.

Beloved, you can also range far beyond your circles and *visit* black folk in schools, jails, and churches. My friends, you should identify a school that you, or your office, or your company, or your peers, might adopt. And then visit that school to share—your insight, resources, or expertise, or just your affirming, concerned presence. Become a mentor and offer career advice to older kids. Offer a word of encouragement to younger kids, too, especially through school counselors who know that black kids must see folk being what they one day wish to become—engineers, lawyers, architects, construction workers, and, yes, firefighters and cops.

You should visit jails and prisons too. I make frequent trips to see my brother in prison, and I also visit other jails and prisons throughout the country. It is an eye-opener. There is a pipeline, my friends, one that runs from classroom to jail, from the playground to the prison. When you visit the incarcerated you'll see how utterly decent most of these men and women are, how they got a bad deal because they were poor with no one to advocate for them.

Visiting a black church is just good for your soul. The best black churches do many of the things that religious folk should be doing if they are concerned about the poor and lost. They set up credit unions for their members. They offer housing for the elderly and the financially strapped. They offer counseling sessions for the mentally beleaguered. They offer ministries to the incarcerated that pay attention as well to the prison industrial complex. Of course when you visit on a Sunday morning, you'll hear the magnificent music of our choirs, the thunderous ways they sing out the joy and wring out the blues by proclaiming faith in God through song. It is contagious.

And you will hear some of the best preaching that the good Lord has ever unleashed on human ears. Many of these ministers are rock stars among the black faithful, and it is here where we benefit from their gifts, giving hope and inspiration to their congregations and leading and loving a people on the precipice of social chaos and urban despair, especially in a time of black-and-blue crisis. The best of them include Freddy Haynes at Friendship-West Baptist Church in Dallas; Lance Watson of St. Paul Baptist in Richmond, Virginia; Alyn Waller at Enon Tabernacle Baptist in Philadelphia; Gina Stewart at Christ Missionary Baptist Church in Memphis; Marcus Cosby at Wheeler Avenue Baptist Church in Houston; Rudolph McKissick at Bethel Baptist Institutional Church in Jacksonville; Otis Moss, III, at Trinity United Church of Christ in Chicago; Jawanza Colvin at Olivet Institutional Baptist Church in Cleveland; Calvin O. Butts, III, at Abyssinian Baptist Church in New York; W. Franklyn Richardson at Grace Baptist in Mt. Vernon, New York; Cynthia Hale at Ray of Hope Christian Church in Atlanta; Vashti McKenzie, the first female elected as bishop in the AME church, serving the state of Texas; and Howard-John Wesley of Alfred Street Baptist Church in Alexandria, Virginia. They tell the truth about black pain and offer abundant inspiration and hope.

Beloved, all of what I have said should lead you to *empathy*. It sounds simple, but its benefits are profound. Whiteness must shed its posture of competence, its will to omniscience, its belief in its goodness and purity, and then walk a mile or two in the boots of blackness. The siege of hate will not end until white folk imagine themselves as black folk—vulnerable despite our virtues. If enough of you, one by one, exercises your civic imagination, and puts yourself in the shoes of your black brothers and sisters, you might develop a democratic impatience for injustice, for the cruel disregard of black life, for the careless indifference to our plight.

Empathy must be cultivated. The practice of empathy means taking a moment to imagine how you might behave if you were in our positions. Do not tell us how we should act if we were you; imagine how you would act if you were us. Imagine living in a society where your white skin marks you for disgust, hate, and fear. Imagine that for many moments. Only when you see black folk as we are, and imagine yourselves as we have to live our lives, only then will the suffering stop, the hurt cease, the pain go away.

VII.
OFFERING PLATE

Besides the crime which consists in violating the law . . . there is commonly injury done to some person or other, and some other man receives damage by his transgression: in which case he who hath received any damage, has, besides the right of punishment common to him with other men, a particular right to seek reparation from him that has done it: and any other person, who finds it just, may also join with him that is injured, and assist him in recovering from the offender so much as may make satisfaction for the harm he has suffered.

—John Locke

Beloved, I was proud to be a member of the Georgetown University faculty in September 2016. Nearly two centuries after the nation's most prominent Jesuit priests sold 272 enslaved human beings to salvage their university's financial future, I sat in Gaston Hall as Georgetown president John DeGioia announced plans to atone for the past. DeGioia said that day that he would offer a formal apology on behalf of the university, establish an institute to study slavery, and erect a public memorial to the slaves who labored to sustain Georgetown, including those men, women, and children—the youngest a two-month-old baby—whose sale in 1838 saved the school. And now, nearly two centuries later, I, an ordained Baptist minister, was the highest-ranking black professor at a Catholic institution that once trafficked in human flesh.

My friends, my pride was tempered by profound grief and anger that any school should rest on the uncompensated labor of folk whose only sin was their skin. It violates every tenet of serious scholarship. It offends every fiber of my being as a black man, as a descendant of enslaved folk in this country.

After DeGioia made his announcement that day, a remarkable thing occurred: history spoke up for itself. Several direct descendants of "the 272," as the enslaved were called, rose to greet the audience and make a statement. They had not been invited to attend, much less expected to speak. But, beloved, the Spirit sometimes moves in mysterious ways.

One of the group members read a prepared document that eloquently expressed their appreciation for Georgetown's efforts to address slavery and its consequences in the present. There was huge applause. And then came off-the-cuff remarks from one of the descendants that were just as powerful, just as affecting. His group, he said, was the face of the suffering endured by their enslaved ancestors. "And our attitude is, 'nothing about us without us.'" He argued that reconciliation couldn't possibly start off by alienating the very descendants of the 272 enslaved the school was honoring. He said they were not seeking reparations, but a partnership to heal the nation's racism.

Beloved, truth is rarely neat. It is often messy. Black truth in white America is especially inconvenient, often not on the program, yet insisting to be heard. To his credit DeGioia showed no hint of defensiveness. He embraced the spirit of partnership that had been extended. DeGioia knows this gesture of atonement is only a start. He knows that offering preferential status in the admissions process to the descendants of the enslaved is just a beginning. Next comes more substantive reckoning with the moral and political consequences of what was done on our hallowed academic ground two centuries ago. The descendant said he wasn't asking for reparations. But, beloved, if we in this nation are to live up to the demands of justice, we should.

VIII.

PRELUDE TO SERVICE

In the early hours of Nov. 9, 2016, the winner of the presidential election was declared . . . All around were the unmistakable signs of normalization in progress. So many were falling into line without being pushed. It was happening at tremendous speed, like a contagion . . . Evil settles into everyday life when people are unable or unwilling to recognize it. It makes its home among us when we are keen to minimize it or describe it as something else. This is not a process that began a week or month or year ago. It did not begin with drone assassinations, or with the war on Iraq. Evil has always been here. But now it has taken on a totalitarian tone.

—Teju Cole

What gives me so much pause, and makes me feel so badly, [is] that the country is willing to be that intolerant and not understand the empathy that's necessary to understand other groups' situations. I'm a rich, white guy. And I'm sick to my stomach thinking about it. I couldn't imagine being a Muslim right now, or a woman, or an African-American, a Hispanic, a handicapped person, and how disenfranchised they might feel. And for anyone in those groups that voted for [Trump], it's just beyond my comprehension how they ignored all that.

— Gregg Popovich

B eloved, the deed has been done. We have—since that "we" must contain, by virtue of our system of government, if not the will, then at least the implied consent, of even the people who opposed with all their souls the choice you made—elected Donald J. Trump as president of the United States of America. Please take measure of every phrase in that sentence. Donald J. Trump, the man who unjustly called into question the citizenship of Barack Obama, our first black president. The man who gave consolation to a gnarled federation of bigots. The man who lent his considerable indignity to berating Muslims, Mexicans, black folk, the other-abled, women, and so many other vulnerable populations. This man has now become the world's most powerful man because he is president of the United States of America, the most powerful nation in history. For millions this is nothing short of a nightmare, or perhaps more accurately, a whitemare.

The election of President Trump was all about whiteness. How whiteness is ingeniously adaptable to a gross variety of circumstances. How it is at once capable of exulting in privilege while proclaiming it is the least privileged of identities. How it is able to hide in plain sight while detesting every other identity that doesn't, and can't, conform to its imperative to invisibility. And how it howls in primal pain at being forgotten while it rushes to spitefully forget and erase all suffering that isn't its own. You will deny it, of course. Already many of those who once bitterly denounced what President Trump stood for have, in startling reversal of their previous positions, embraced the possibility of his goodness, or, at least, his fitful utility, a trend that will no doubt continue into the future.

My friends, the mistake we often make is to believe that whiteness is only prejudice, that it is only bigotry, that it is only racism, that it is only the cry of hate. That is only partly true. The other part of whiteness is the delusion that it can supply every need that our country has. Both of these impulses suffocate the vitality of democracy. Beloved, Donald Trump is what we are left with when whiteness drains the body politic of crucial self-awareness and we stiffen into a moral corpse.

When the defenders of whiteness proclaim that it is not whiteness that was at stake in electing Trump, but, instead, the ache of poverty and class, what they mostly always fail to mention is that millions of black and brown folk are poor, or working class, too. It is only the white lower and middle classes whose silent suffering is portrayed as having got a president elected. As important as their economic vulnerability is, it is not the major engine of their disgust; rather it is the fury of whiteness unleashed, of whiteness unbounded, of whiteness made, not less white, but even whiter by its class rage, a rage that oddly leaves aside solidarity with millions of other hurting souls whose only reason for exclusion is their color.

Beloved, when the defenders of whiteness argue that the white folk who supported candidate Trump were not magnetized by his miserably shining hatefulness toward so many "others," they defy the physics of race and the algorithm of bigotry. There is a fairly easy calculus to racism: if it increases, rather than decreases, the force, energy, and structure of racial antagonism, then it is racist, no matter the intent or conscious aim of its perpetrator.

Many white folk, including the wealthy, and the surprising numbers of women who voted for him, whether they can admit it or not, were attracted to candidate Trump, not because he wasn't President Obama, which is a reasonable political choice, but because he wasn't the black man who had taken their country. "Make America Great Again" is hardly coded, and not primarily, or merely, a brilliantly deceptive campaign slogan, but a sturdy credo, and the gist of faith in whiteness. To "Make America Great Again" is in truth to make America white again. Some might argue that that can't possibly be the case. After all, America twice elected Obama to the presidency. Yet we fail to see that a majority of white folk never liked Obama and never wanted him as their president. They never invited him, metaphorically, into their homes. The majority of white folk just got outvoted twice.

Beloved, a massive white rebellion was fomented in our midst, a rebellion driven by resentment of a black man in charge, resentment, too, of the widely perceived, yet grossly exaggerated, black benefit under Obama—that black folk got an unfair leg up, all because, finally, for the first time in 220 years, a black man darkened the Oval Office. It is hard to overstate just how poisonous Obama was believed to be in the precincts of a spurning, rebutting whiteness, a whiteness that measured the seconds until he would no longer be in that white house, in our, or rather, their, White House. Millions of whites couldn't wait to return power to the white hands from which it had been cruelly snatched for eight years, couldn't wait to celebrate the victory of the most brazenly white man to claim the presidency since Andrew Johnson.

Beloved, there is a truth to Trump's election that many of you refuse to see: too many white folk are willing to imperil the ship of state because they lust for revenge. It is, in truth, *wevenge,* the unrepentant mutiny of a rogue white crew. They seem willing to cast aside a seasoned leader because of her gender, and her connection to the previous captain. Instead, they have embraced a fatally inexperienced skipper who threatens to wreck the vaunted vessel of government in the rocky waters of political ignorance.

Whether he wishes to be or not, Donald Trump is the epitome, not only of white innocence and white privilege, but of white power, white rage, and, yes, even of white supremacy.

The greatly stepped-up harassment of people of color, and Muslims, and immigrants in the wake of Trump's election points to the sea change in our naked tolerance for such assaults, in the permission granted to diabolical forces that rob us even more of comity and support of the commonweal.

Donald Trump harms our nation's positive racial future.

Yet, beloved, there remains, after all, the blackness that is prophecy, the blackness that is inexplicable hope in the face of savage hopelessness. The great black prophet and mystic Howard Thurman says it best.

At the time when the slaves in America were without any excuse for hope and they could see nothing before them but the long interminable cotton rows and the fierce sun and the lash of the overseer, what did they do? They declared that God was not through. They said, "We cannot be prisoners of this event. We must not scale down the horizon of our hopes and our dreams and our yearnings to the level of the event of our lives." So they lived through their tragic moment until at last they came out on the other side, saluting the fulfillment of their hopes and their faith.

Beloved, if the enslaved could nurture, on the vine of their desperate deficiency of democracy, the spiritual and moral fruit that fed our civilization, then surely we can name and resist demagoguery; we can protest, and somehow defeat, the forces that threaten the soul of our nation. To not try, to give up on the possibility that we can make a difference, can make *the* difference, is to give up on our past, on our complicated, difficult, but victorious past. Donald Trump is not our final, or ultimate, problem. The problem is, instead, allowing hopelessness to steal our joyful triumph before we work hard enough to achieve it.

IX.

CLOSING PRAYER

Everything want to be loved. Us sing and dance and hol-ler, just trying to be loved.

—Alice Walker, *The Color Purple*

Oh God, the hour is dark. The suffering is great. But we will not give up. We will not surrender.

We will not surrender because we have endured the lash of spite and the whip of hate on our backs.

We will not surrender because we know that faith is greater than fear, good triumphant over evil, love more noble than hate.

We will not surrender because our mothers and fathers, and their mothers and fathers, and their mothers and fathers, and their mothers and fathers, too, believed in you, believed in us, believed that no obstacle put in their way could stop them. They believed that the grace you gave them for their journeys would outlast any challenge to their hearts and minds.

We will not surrender because your enduring and indestructible Word feeds the souls of our people.

We will not surrender because blackness is a gift that has blessed the world beyond compare. Our minds and hearts, and our tongues and bodies, too, have made Earth a better place to live. We will not surrender because we have survived.

Oh God, we are not naïve. We know, just as white America knows, that our legion, multiple, complicated, adaptable, triumphant blackness threatens whiteness.

Oh God, you placed a paradox in our midst like a rainbow at the end of a storm: if we are to understand America we must understand blackness.

Oh Lord, black folk are everything; we are every possibility of American, even human, identity made real. That means we are everywhere, just like our white brothers and sisters.

We are going nowhere. We are your children too. We will survive. We are America.

SUNDAY SCHOOL
LESSONS

Discussion questions:

1. The book is structured as a sermon. How does that impact your reading? Would a traditional narrative structure have worked as well?
2. Did the book change your thinking in any way?
3. Do you have friends of different races? Why or why not?
4. How does the use of music in the second chapter, "Hymns of Praise," create a chorus that further strengthens the argument?
5. In the "Invocation," Dyson's voice changes as he simultaneously begs for forgiveness and defends his actions. Why does Dyson take this voice, and what does it invoke in you?
6. What alternate history does Dyson present in the "Scripture Reading," and how does it conflict with the "history" accepted by many Americans?
7. Is whiteness an invention?
8. Why does the statement Black Lives Matter make so many people so angry?
9. How does Dyson restructure the responsibility of understanding and combating racism?
10. What is white fragility and how does it hinder constructive communication surrounding race?
11. Does every white person have white privilege?
12. In "The Plague of White Innocence," Dyson states, "Justice is what love sounds like when it speaks in public." What does he mean by that?

13. If someone uses a racial slur in your presence, how do you react?

14. Throughout the book, Dyson dedicates stories to destabilizing white American "truths." In "Coptopia," what "truths" does he say that police represent to white Americans? How do Dyson's memories break down those "truths"?

15. How do we work with local, state, and federal governments to prevent violence against people of color?

16. What actions can you take in your private and work life to combat institutional racism?

17. What are reparations? If reparations were adopted and approved by federal and state governments, what forms do you think they'd take?

18. Is it unpatriotic to refuse to stand for the National Anthem?

ABOUT THE AUTHOR

© KK Ottesen

MICHAEL ERIC DYSON—distinguished University Professor of African American and Diaspora Studies, College of Arts & Science, and of Ethics and Society, Divinity School, and Centennial Professor at Vanderbilt University—is one of America's premier public intellectuals and the author of seven *New York Times* bestsellers, including *JAY-Z*, *Tears We Cannot Stop*, and *What Truth Sounds Like*, and most recently *Long Time Coming*. A contributing opinion writer for *The New York Times*, Dr. Dyson is a recipient of two NAACP Image awards and the 2020 Langston Hughes Festival Medallion. Former president Barack Obama has noted: "Everybody who speaks after Michael Eric Dyson pales in comparison."